Fighting Spirit

Embracing life beyond diagnosis with will, hope and optimism

Belinda Borrelli

Charlie and Meghan

May you find some hope and inspiration in the pages of this story as you journey through life. Wishing that you continue your world travels and live life to its fullest!

Love and much thanks for your support.

Sincerely
Belinda Borrelli
08-27-25

Photographs in chapter 8, pages 118-119 by Dana Cole Photography.
Photographs in chapter 14, page 206 by DeLuca Films.

Library and Archives Canada Cataloguing in Publication

CIP data on file with the National Library and Archives

ISBN 978-1-55483-594-2 (trpb)
ISBN 978-1-55483-595-9 (e-book)

This book is dedicated to:

Dr. Rodrigo Bagur who strongly encouraged me to tell my story to inspire and give hope to others, thus becoming the impetus for this memoir.

My children, Jenna and Justin, who have provided me with meaning and purpose.

My guardian angel, Jordan, who continues to watch over me.

My husband, Dan, who has been my pillar of strength, my best friend and my soulmate. We travelled this journey together, as I could not have done it without your unwavering support and your love. From the beginning, you have been my rock.

Contents

Contents

Foreword

It is not often that a surgeon is invited to reflect upon the journey of a patient, especially one who has experienced such an extraordinary series of life-threatening medical challenges. As I sit to write this foreword, I am deeply honoured and privileged to share in the unfolding of this story that transcends the typical medical journey – a narrative not only of survival, but one of resilience, courage, and an unyielding spirit. Despite fifty years of operating on patients with life-threatening conditions, I continue to be humbled and inspired by the courage and resilience of the human spirit.

Since 1987, I have had the privilege of being involved in Belinda's medical odyssey from its inception. I have witnessed firsthand the trials she has faced and the remarkable way she has navigated through each of them. Over the past four decades, she has had to confront five different life-threatening conditions, each requiring specialized medical and surgical interventions. Yet, despite the gravity of each of these challenges, she has not only fought with overwhelming strength, but with the unwavering support of her loving family. She embraced the process with hope, courage, determination, and a willingness to learn, adapt and thrive, even in the face of overwhelming odds.

This book is not just an account of surgeries and medical diagnoses; it is a testament to Belinda's fortitude, determined fighting spirit and the invaluable relationships she has forged with her healthcare providers. Beyond the medical struggles endured by this remarkable individual, this memoir is a reminder of what truly matters in life – personal connection, hope, and the relentless pursuit of life, no matter the challenges that lie ahead. This book is a tribute to the human condition – vulnerable, fragile, and resilient. It is a story of one person's journey, yes, but it speaks to all of us, reminding us of our strength in the face of adversity.

Just as I have, may you, the reader, find inspiration in these pages; may you come away with a deeper appreciation for the quiet warriors among us, whose stories of survival deserve to be heard, remembered, celebrated and impressed on all of us that the human spirit is capable of enduring more than we ever thought possible.

Dr. Gaetano DeRose, BSc, MD, FRCS (C), FACS
Professor Emeritus, Department of Surgery
Western University,
London, Ontario, Canada

Preface

This is my raw and untold personal story to share. I hope it will resonate with you – the highs and lows, the challenges and triumphs in health and life. I wish it will inspire and strengthen you to fight through life's adversities and bring hope that you can overcome them.

The idea for writing this memoir began on a typical autumn day in November 2023. Prior to my impending open-heart surgery, I was required to undergo an angiogram procedure at the London Health Sciences Centre – University Hospital to determine if I had any heart blockages. It was then that I first met a very personable cardiologist, Dr. Rodrigo Bagur.

As I was being readied for the procedure, Dr. Bagur came to my side and patted my shoulder. In Italian, he asked me if I spoke Italian. In Italian, I replied, "Yes, a little." Then again in Italian, he asked me how I was doing. This time, I responded in English and said, "I'm doing pretty well, thanks." My response in English elicited a chuckle from him.

"I speak in Italian, and you respond in English?" he exclaimed.

I remember being so impressed with how he began our first encounter, and I told him so. He replied, "I know that our patients come in nervous and anxious and I just try to reassure them and break the ice."

Once the angiogram was complete, I was wheeled to the recovery room to wait with my husband, Dan, to receive the results of the testing. A short time later, Dr. Bagur came in and gave us the unfortunate news that I had another narrowing of the right coronary artery slightly above the area where they had inserted a stent six years prior. He indicated that in addition to correcting three heart valves, he would now be recommending to my heart surgeon, Dr. Michael Chu, that a bypass of the right coronary artery was necessary.

We felt dejected and demoralized but not unsurprised. Dan and I knew clearly that this meant an additional hurdle to overcome during the open-heart surgery I was scheduled to undergo a month later. We sensed Dr. Bagur's regret in sharing this news with us.

"I have one last thing to tell you," he said.

Our eyes lowered and our jaws dropped. Dan and I wondered, "What next?"

Dr. Bagur looked at me to tell me, "You have been a true inspiration, considering everything you have been through in your life. I am giving you an assignment. I am asking you to write a book about your journey so that you can inspire and give hope to others as they go through their health challenges."

Our eyes welled up, I knew what both Dan and I were thinking. This doctor gets it; he understands what we have been through.

Dr. Bagur then held my hand, and the last thing I remember him saying was, "Remember that, yes, I am a cardiologist. But I am a human being first." What a powerful and telling message he left us with.

Unquestionably, Dr. Bagur, you sowed the seeds for writing my story. I have completed the work you assigned to me that November day. I dedicate this to you.

Chapter 1

The "C" Word

In May 1987, I had almost completed a full year of occasional teaching. I received a call from the Windsor Catholic District School Board indicating that they wanted to offer me a full-time high school teaching position beginning four months later in September. Ecstatic and without hesitation, I hurried to the board office. I signed all of the required documents and paperwork, and I prepared myself to begin my first full-time teaching experience.

The following month, in June, surprisingly, a second small mass caught my attention just above my left collarbone. You see, the year before, I had detected an enlarged single lymph node above my right collarbone. I brought it to the attention of my family doctor who sent me for a chest X-ray. The X-ray came back negative, and I didn't give it a second thought, until I found that second node. My family doctor once again sent me for an X-ray, and in addition, he then referred me to a surgeon for a consultation.

After a consultation with the surgeon, he indicated nonchalantly that he would 'pop the node out' and send it for testing. To be honest, I never suspected anything was wrong. I was 25 years old, feeling healthy, and life was going well. It was early July of the same year when I was booked to have the lymph node removed in a room next to the surgeon's examination room. Dan sat apprehensively outside in the waiting area.

The doctor froze the area around the right collarbone and began cutting into the skin. I was nervous and fully aware of what was going on. Immediately, I felt blood trickling down my neck. I then felt the tugging and tearing of the tissue as he 'popped out the node.' Not only could I feel the tugging and tearing sensations, but I could hear them. It was as if raw animal meat was being ripped off of a bone. When the removal was finally completed, I was swiftly stitched back up. The entire procedure left me distressed. Visibly shaken, I waited a few minutes to regain my bearings and was escorted to the waiting area to meet up with Dan. The experience was daunting and worse than what I was expecting. I walked to the waiting area, white as a ghost and in significant pain. My head was noticeably tilted sideways, and I felt as if a wedge had been cut out of my neck.

Just prior to me leaving the surgical area, the surgeon left the room, vial in hand filled with the excised node. Unbeknownst to me, Dan quickly approached the surgeon and asked him if the node looked normal. The surgeon replied, "It looks normal for the abnormal." Staggered, Dan knew something was not right, but the surgeon gave no further clues. The surgeon specified that Dan would have to wait for the pathology report to be completed.

Hodgkin Lymphoma

Dan was off work for a few days to take care of me as I recovered. Slowly, I felt the so-called wedge in my neck reduce in size and I began to feel better. A few evenings later, I insisted that Dan return to work, but he was adamant that he was going to stay with me for at least another day. I kept insisting that he return to work, but to no avail.

Dan then quietly said, "Belinda, sit down." With sadness reflected on his face, he continued, "I have something to tell you."

At this point, I got a little nervous, and could start to feel my heart pounding, but despite that, I sat down at the edge of our bed.

Eyes starting to water, Dan proceeded, "I don't know how to tell you." He paused for a moment but what seemed like an eternity. I anxiously waited. He slowly got the words out, "You have cancer."

My heart sank. I felt a jolt as if I had been gut-punched. Suddenly, an unexplained weakness came over me.

He continued, "I stopped at the family doctor's office, and he went over the pathology report with me. I am so, so sorry to tell you that you have a cancer called Hodgkin Lymphoma."

An unwelcome feeling of sadness filled the room. The news unleashed so many emotions: shock, daze and confusion. I couldn't believe what I was hearing. "Are you sure?" I questioned. "How could this be?" I wondered. "But I feel so good," I confirmed. I felt as if the rug had been pulled out from under me.

Dan gave me a warm hug, and together, we shed our tears. After retreating from the shocking news, I tried to process the information. As I gradually settled into a new unknown, Dan and I knew that we needed to try to get some rest. We understood that there would be a good deal of work ahead of us, and we wanted to be prepared. Suddenly, a new chapter of dealing with life began.

Neither of us slept that evening. There were so many thoughts going through my mind – some were positive, many were negative. I kept thinking of my sister getting married in less than four weeks. I wondered how I would break this shocking news to my parents, to my sister, Cindy, and to my younger 13-year-old brother, Michael, who wouldn't even really know what cancer was. I questioned whether I could start my new teaching role in less than two months. Worse yet, would I even be alive?

We contemplated how and when to break the news to my parents, my sister and brother. I knew they would be as shocked and destroyed as Dan and I were when we first learned of the diagnosis. What I did know was that I wanted to keep the news under wraps for the next four weeks, until after my sister's wedding, so as not to overshadow her special day. After meeting with the oncologist the following week, we uneasily decided we had little choice. As difficult as it would be, we would let my family know that evening.

It was a warm July evening, and Dan and I settled on telling my mom and dad while the four of us were out on a walk. We started with some small talk, but quickly got into the real reason for our discussion. Explaining to a parent that their child had cancer, regardless of age, would be devastating and my parents were no different. I knew they would be crushed by the news. I felt anxious, but with my heart racing and my legs weak, Dan and I proceeded, as gently as possible, to tell them of my diagnosis. As expected, they were shocked and in disbelief. Dan and I kept repeating and reassuring them that I would be alright. I did believe that I was going to come out of this successfully, even though negative thoughts continually fogged my mind.

When we returned home, we knew it was time to break the news to my sister and brother. Once again, we proceeded as delicately as possible to reveal our newly found information. We quietly broke the news to them that I had cancer. They didn't quite know how to react or process the news, but they would each find their way to handle it. We wanted all of my family to know that we wished to keep it quiet until after my sister's wedding.

Within the next few days, we had an appointment at the Metropolitan Hospital – Cancer Clinic in Windsor, Ontario with our new oncologist. As I walked anxiously through the doors of the cancer clinic for the first time, reality set in. I confirmed to myself, "The cancer victim is me."

In that moment, I needed a dose of empathy and understanding and my oncologist was there to offer that. She reassured us that if I had to get cancer, Hodgkin's was the best one to get. She confidently emphasized that the odds for a five-year survival rate were in our favour, as shown in Table 1. She also explained to us that the course of treatment would be dependent upon the extent of the cancer, known as the 'staging of the disease.' Feeling overwhelmed and distracted, I refocused. Apparently, in 1987, the staging process could only be done through several tests and major surgery called a staging laparotomy. This procedure would determine how far the cancer had spread. A number of those required tests were ordered and scheduled as well. The latest diagnostics had not advanced that far, and PET scans or other less invasive methods were not available at that time.

Table 1
Hodgkin Lymphoma Survival

Stage	5-year relative survival
1	90%
2	90%
3	80%
4	65%

Note. Adapted from https://cancer.ca/en/cancer-information/cancer-types/hodgkin-lymphoma/prognosis-and-survival/survival-statistics. Copyright (2023) by Canadian Cancer Society.

Staging the Disease

With the approaching crucial surgery, our experiences with doctors, nurses and many other healthcare providers were about to begin. Dan and I knew that surgery was a big part of the diagnostics, and except for the removal of my wisdom teeth, I had never been put under a general anesthetic. Dan wanted to find an experienced, trusted surgeon with a good track record in discovering, as accurately as possible, findings to properly stage the Hodgkin Lymphoma.

This is when we solicited the help of Dan's brother, Paul. Paul had a friend, originally from Windsor, who was now a vascular surgeon in London, Ontario. Paul put us in contact with Dr. Guy DeRose. Little did Dr. DeRose know how integral a part he would play in our lives, especially in my most critical and vulnerable moments. From this point forward, the kind, soft-spoken and humble Dr. DeRose never left our side and, to this day, he has travelled our journey alongside us.

Dr. DeRose referred us to the trusted, knowledgeable and well-respected surgeon we were looking for, Dr. David Girvan, from London. A consultation was set up with the surgeon, and we were scheduled to meet with him a week later. My worried and concerned mom had a strong desire to learn as much as she could about what was going on with me. Whenever possible, she wanted to be included in any doctors' meetings and tests or treatment plans. Hence, she asked to be present at the consultation with Dr. Girvan. With three weeks to go until my sister's wedding, Dan, my mom and I headed for London the following week.

Dr. Girvan was a very professional, mild-mannered and compassionate doctor who empathized with me and my family. He explained in detail what he would be doing during the surgery: testing random lymph nodes in the abdominal area, biopsy the liver and pelvic bone marrow and biopsy and remove the spleen. He made it clear that the accuracy rate of what would be discovered in the staging laparotomy would be approximately 95%. In other words, because every lymph node could not possibly be tested, there would always be a small chance that cancerous cells might go undetected.

Dr. Girvan indicated that his first availability was the following month, on August 5. Without hesitation, my mom and Dan jumped at accepting that date and immediately told the surgeon to book it. Nevertheless, Dr. Girvan cordially looked at the three of us and indicated that we should check with the patient first. It took me a few seconds, but I knew that the date worked out well. I still had time to undergo preliminary testing allowing me to be present at my sister's wedding on August 1. I looked at my mom and Dan, and then I turned to Dr. Girvan and asked if he could schedule that open date.

The next few weeks were a whirlwind of activity between completing final preparations for the wedding, meeting with my oncologist and undergoing a battery of tests. One of the medical tests involved making a small incision on the top of each of my feet to allow for the insertion of a tiny tube. Following the procedure, the incisions were then covered with a tiny bandage. I was pleased that the bandages looked inconspicuous. Given that I would be wearing a cocktail-length dress at the wedding, I did not want to call attention to my feet. As I stated earlier, I wanted to keep my illness under wraps until the wedding had passed, so I wanted to avoid unnecessary questions. Ironically, the wedding preparations became a welcome diversion from the cancer diagnosis. Those few weeks provided us with a healthy balance of days of trepidation mixed with exciting times.

The long-awaited August 1 wedding finally arrived. After the ceremony, I unexpectedly received several comments and questions about what I thought were small, inconspicuous bandages. I laughed with the guests, and I hastily changed the subject. As quickly as the day arrived, the event flew by and went off without a hitch. When the evening drew to a close, I could feel myself struggling with reality. Sadness, disappointment and fear steadily crept into my thoughts. Up to this point, the wedding was a distraction from the illness, but now, once again, I was forced to face the diagnosis and the pending surgery. At that moment, Dan and I were relieved that the news of the diagnosis remained relatively silent, and my family, especially my sister, was able to enjoy the event undisturbed from any outside elements.

Beginning the following day, Dan and I started to break the news to our close extended family and good friends. We would be travelling to London for surgery a mere two days later. Was it difficult and taxing to repeat the sad news over and over? Definitely. Nonetheless, we felt the need to share the information personally as it was to the people who meant so much to us and deserved to receive the news directly from Dan and me.

It was the morning of August 5, I tried to prepare myself both physically and mentally for surgery day. We had travelled to London the previous day, and I was able to get settled into what would become my new *home* for the next week or so. The morning of surgery, I was feeling particularly nervous and anxious, especially as I wondered what Dr. Girvan would discover during surgery.

The nurses carefully prepared me for the procedure, gowning me up, inserting an IV and placing a cap on my head. As one of my nurses covered my hair with the cap, she took care to neatly place my hair under the cap. She then said to me, "I don't want to mess your hair." It seemed like such a small gesture but what the nurse did and said helped to put me at ease – that meant a great deal to me.

I was then all set and ready for surgery. Dan and I waited for our time. My scheduled surgery time came and went, and we continued to patiently wait. Finally, a nurse came into my room to apologetically tell me that Dr. Girvan was called in to do an emergency surgery on a young child who had been in an accident. Unfortunately, my surgery would need to be postponed to the following day.

Dan and I were disappointed and deflated, but we fully understood the gravity of the situation and the need to prioritize the urgent occurrence. Later that same evening, much to our surprise, Dan and I received a visit from Dr. Girvan. Just imagine, he came to personally apologize for having to reschedule the surgery until the following day. Considerate actions like that resonated with us. We would come to experience and greatly appreciate many more of these similar acts of kindness by our healthcare professionals, and we cannot begin to tell you how much that meant to us.

The next morning, I awoke in a different frame of mind. I was relaxed, calm and at peace with what was about to take place. In much the same way as the previous day, I was prepared for surgery. I put my gown on, the IV was inserted, and a cap was placed over my hair. Dan kissed me goodbye, said, "I love you," and I was gently wheeled to the operating room.

The next thing I knew, I came out of surgery in the recovery room. I remember feeling intense pain all over my abdominal area and just above the groin. It felt as if my organs had been ripped out. I worriedly thought to myself that Dr. Girvan must have needed to open up all of my insides. I apologized repeatedly to the nurses for making such a fuss about the pain, but they reassured me that I was not complaining. Through all the pain, I felt comforted by the care and compassion shown in recovery. It certainly helped to ease the discomfort.

When I was finally wheeled back to my room, there were several family visitors waiting to see me. They believed that I had the surgery the previous day and, in their minds, I was one day post-surgery. In reality, I was still quite sedated and groggy following the very recent surgery. After some short visits, my room cleared, and Dan and I waited for Dr. Girvan to give us an update.

Shortly thereafter, Dr. Girvan came into my room to give Dan and me preliminary results. Even waiting a few seconds for the doctor's next words seemed like an eternity. Dan and I would realize that no matter how many times we would find ourselves in that decisive moment, it would never get any easier. We knew those next words could forever change our lives, and we held our breaths. Fortunately, and with a great deal of comfort, he let us know that the surgery went well and that, as far as he could see, there were no enlarged lymph nodes. The pathology results of the areas that were biopsied would follow a few days later, but again, Dr. Girvan indicated that, at that point, nothing looked suspicious. Dan and I breathed a huge sigh of relief.

In the week that followed in the hospital, I slowly recovered from the surgery, trying to abide by the instructions given to me: breathing exercises to prevent pneumonia, walking exercises to improve circulation and weight-bearing exercises to improve strength. With each passing day, the pain improved as did my strength and circulation.

Pathology Results

Within that week, Dr. Girvan returned to speak to us about the pathology results. Again, we waited with bated breath. Within seconds, he reassuringly stated that the random nodes that were tested, including the liver, spleen and bone marrow biopsies, all came back negative. Based on all of the testing, it appeared that the cancer had not spread below the chest area. Dan and I heaved a long sigh of relief. That was the best news we could have hoped for! Although, we knew that this was only the beginning. We knew that upon our return to Windsor, I would need to meet with an oncologist to determine the course of treatment required to conquer the disease.

Upon being discharged from the hospital, I received medication and information sheets. Also, I was given an appointment form to return to Dr. Girvan's office for a six-week follow-up. Then I realized that the follow-up appointment would take me into the second week of the new school year.

When Dan and I returned to Windsor around mid-August, I took it easy and afforded my body time to heal. On the other hand, I was due to begin my first-ever teaching assignment in about three weeks. The thought of starting my teaching career in that short timeframe was unsettling. I had a great deal of work to do to properly prepare myself, and I was not at one hundred percent yet, not even close.

My appointment with the Windsor Regional Cancer Clinic was to take place the week following my return from London. My mom, wanting to be well-informed, asked if she could accompany us to that appointment. Therefore, that week, Dan, my mom and I met with a radiation oncologist. We had an in-depth consultation with the oncologist as he detailed several things about the actual disease and how far the cancer had spread. Based on the pathology reports from the surgery, the oncologist explained that I had Stage 2 Hodgkin Lymphoma. As originally thought, this confirmed that I had cancerous cells in the neck and chest area. In discussion with the rest of his oncology team, radiation was the recommended course of treatment.

The recommendation of treating the cancer with radiation had to do mainly with my age. If I were older and had already bore children, the encompassing treatment would have been chemotherapy. Conversely, at 25 years of age, the odds of me conceiving following the prescribed chemotherapy regimen, rested at 50%. Additionally, in 1987 the option of freezing eggs for future fertilization was not available. Therefore, ironically, the science pointed toward treating the lymphoma with radiation therapy, thereby minimizing the harmful effects of chemotherapy.

At that time, in our minds, Dan and I were very relieved that I was recommended for radiation therapy and not chemotherapy. This would include 20 sessions of radiation to the chest area, known as mantle radiation followed by a 20-day rest period with no radiation and then ending with another 20 sessions of radiation to the upper abdomen area. We also consulted with Dr. Girvan's radiation oncologist in London to get a second opinion. She concurred with Windsor's course of treatment and verified that the London Cancer Centre would have recommended the same treatment plan. Therefore, Dan and I decided to undergo radiation treatments in Windsor.

Forging Ahead

Initial Thoughts

When I first began writing this memoir, I didn't want it to be a sorrowful account of the health issues that I faced. I wanted it to be a story of encouragement and a beacon of hope for people facing life's adversities. Each one of us will face challenges in our lives. We will each have our cross to bear – some sooner, some later, some lighter, some heavier. Undoubtedly, in varying degrees, we will all encounter suffering at different points throughout our lives. It is what we do when faced with these challenges that truly define us.

Following my initial diagnosis of Hodgkin Lymphoma, I rode this roller coaster of emotions – shock, disbelief, fear – but on the other hand, I felt hope, belief and motivation. Also, deep down inside, I felt that there might be a reason why I was afflicted with this disease. I shared this thought with Dan. Perhaps there was an underlying message that I needed to carry out. It was a fleeting thought in my mind and only time would tell.

Reflecting back and without realizing it at that time, that cancer diagnosis would become the seed that fostered my personal growth from that point forward.

Self motivation was a key factor in helping me to overcome my challenge. One thing that motivated me in battling this disease was looking for inspiration from others. One such person was my mother's cousin, who lived in a suburb of Toronto, Ontario. About 14 years prior to my diagnosis, she, too, was diagnosed with Hodgkin Lymphoma. She attended her sister's wedding during her chemotherapy treatments with her wig in place. On that wedding day, I witnessed her taking her illness in stride and 'living life to its fullest.' I remember looking up to her and being impressed with how she handled her illness. Little did I know that I would be walking in her shoes 14 years later.

Currently faced with the same disease as my relative, I often looked back to that moment and felt encouraged. I thought, "If she can do it, so can I." She became my motivation to beat this disease. She did not dwell on the challenges she endured. Instead, she faced her health issues head-on and displayed a positive attitude and a vibrant outlook on life, smiling along the way. As an aside, that wedding day took place about 50 years ago, and she is still enjoying life to this day.

I did not want my disease to stop me from living. I wanted life to continue for Dan's sake, for my parents' sake and for the sake of my family and friends, even though few people knew at that time. After the diagnosis and prior to my sister's wedding, Dan and I continued to watch my brother's baseball games at our local diamonds, attended family functions, and participated in all the pre-wedding activities. It was important for us to live life as normally as possible and not to waste life's precious moments. I believed, "Life is for the living. Live it to its fullest."

Another important driving force to help Dan and me was knowledge. Knowledge is power. From the onset of the diagnosis, Dan needed to find out as much information as he could about the disease, the course of recommended treatments available and survival statistics. Dan felt knowledge was power no matter how good or bad the acquired information generated. You have to remember that in 1987, there was no Internet. At that time, the source of information for lay people was journal articles in large book volume form. Dan quickly sought the help of a few nurses at the cancer clinic in Windsor. Together, they spent time in the clinic library researching relevant articles about Hodgkin's disease. He made copies of the articles, and would take them home to read. To this day, Dan is very inquisitive, curious and thirsty for knowledge on the current health issue we are facing.

That August, while recovering from the surgery, I was nervously thinking about starting my new career in teaching and knew that I could not do it alone. The beginning of the new academic year was about three weeks away and I had a great deal of work to properly prepare myself. Firstly, I had to take things slowly to recover fully.

And secondly, I needed to take time to meet with veteran teachers to learn the curriculum and to begin planning units of study. Time was not on my side.

In the three-week lead-up to the start of my first school year, I connected with newly met colleagues to help me navigate my teaching assignments. I met with my department head several times and I met with other teachers in my department. My department head was so understanding and empathetic at a time when support was much needed. He provided me with as many resources as he could to get me started for the new courses I would soon be teaching. My colleagues were very supportive and helped me in whatever way possible. I do not know if they fully understood the valuable impact that their experience, expertise and guidance had on me as a novice teacher.

The school year quickly approached, and I began week one by establishing new routines in my life. I started the school year before returning to Dr. Girvan for my six-week follow-up. For those who don't know me, there would be little to stop me from going to work, especially for my first full-time teaching assignment. In my second week, it was mandatory to take a day off of work so that Dan and I could drive to London for my six-week checkup appointment with Dr. Girvan.

The doctor was pleased with how I was progressing in my recovery and overall, everything went well in that appointment. Dan and I returned to Windsor so that I could resume my teaching responsibilities. In addition, it was time to prepare myself for another new schedule and the start of my radiation treatments.

In that same second week of teaching, the principal called me into his office. He explained that, coincidentally, a then current 15-year-old student in grade 9 at our school was also recently diagnosed with Hodgkin Lymphoma. He asked if I would be willing to speak to her and her parents about my experiences to alleviate some of their fears and concerns and to provide them with some reassurance in these difficult times. I had just gone through this a few months ago, so I had a vivid memory of what Dan and I had just experienced. Of course, we would talk to her and her parents. The message that went through my mind was, 'Be kind and think of others who are suffering.' If our story and experiences could help someone else,

then we would do it.

Radiation Treatments Begin

It was the third week of the school year, and I was due to begin my radiation treatments on a Monday. I would be going to the radiation department of the cancer clinic, Mondays to Fridays, for four weeks. Prior to my first session, I had X-rays taken to accurately locate the positioning of my heart, lungs and any other affected areas in the radiation field that could be potentially damaging to these organs. Lead blocks, closely resembling the shape of my organs were produced to be used during my radiation treatments to protect both the chest and upper abdomen areas.

When the treatments began, and with each subsequent session, the radiology technologist lowered a Plexiglas surface toward my chest. She then meticulously placed lead blocks on the Plexiglas – one to protect the heart, a second and third to protect the lungs and on any other areas requiring protection. In a very short amount of time, the radiation was emitted, lead blocks were removed, and the Plexiglas was raised. The preparation time took the longest, but otherwise, it was a quick and painless process.

I never pretended that the entire radiation treatment would be an easy endeavour. One of the most challenging parts was to get myself to the cancer clinic by 3 p.m., the last appointment time. Our school's dismissal time was 2:35 p.m. I would have to pack up all of my books and binders at the end of my last class each day, rush to my car at bell time and drive the required seven kilometres to the clinic, find a place to park and register at the radiation department before 3 p.m. As silly as it sounds, never did I imagine that this routine would become one of the most anxious pieces of the entire radiation treatment process.

To make matters worse, on one specific occasion, after rushing to the cancer clinic, I dutifully completed my radiation treatment. Following the timely procedure, I left the clinic to attend my brother's high school playoff volleyball match. The school was located just a short distance from the clinic. On my drive, I made a left turn from the main street onto the side street to reach the high school. As I was making the left turn, I quickly noticed the sign on the post from the corner of my eye. Yes, the No Left Turn sign. I immediately figured that I was within the prohibited time frame, but I hoped that I was not spotted. Seconds later, I was stopped by an officer on his motorcycle. I thought about using the cancer card, but I decided against it. Discouragingly, I accepted the ticket. Thus, not only was it hectic getting to the clinic on time, but I found out the hard way that it was also nerve-wracking leaving it.

Without a doubt, leaving school at bell time, especially as a new teacher, was stressful and not pleasant for me. I would have preferred to have taken my time to review what I had covered that day, plan for the next day's lessons and complete any required tasks. On a lighter note, not only would I have wanted more time after school, I would have also preferred to have read street signs properly when returning from the clinic. Nevertheless, life is all relative. When faced with adversity, you do what you have to do.

Looking back on that year, as I faced my first real health challenge in life, I encountered a wide range of feelings. It was an emotional roller coaster ride, one that I was relieved to get off of. Little did I know at that time that I would be getting back on that ride over and over again.

My passion for travel began early. At 9 months of age, while visiting my relatives in Treviso, Veneto, Italy, my uncle had this picture taken of me.

Enjoying an active life, my sister Cindy and I are ready for our figure skating show.

On August 18, 1984, I married my best friend, Dan. Pictured are my mom, Aldina, my dad, Bruno, my sister, Cindy and my brother, Michael.

On the shores of Lake Superior, Dan and I shared a moment of reflection. Not long after, our lives would be turned upside down as we would soon face the onset of health challenges.

Chapter 2

The Big "C" Returns

After completing 20 sessions of radiation therapy to the chest area, I was given a four-week break before starting my final 20 sessions to the upper abdomen. I welcomed that four-week break as I did not have to endure the daily regimen of the radiation treatment process. In addition, I was able to put off the tight timeline challenge for even four weeks. It was a stress reliever to take my time after school. I was able to stay later to update my daily planner, plan lessons for the following day and take care of any unfinished tasks.

That four-week break ended as quickly as it started. Before I knew it, I was back at the cancer clinic's radiation department to complete my final sessions of radiation. The process would be similar to the radiation treatments of the chest area that were administered four to eight weeks prior. The only exception was that lead blocks were reproduced and now used to protect any potentially damaging areas of the upper abdomen. Again, I had to arrive at the cancer clinic by 3 p.m. The treatments would be administered in much the same fashion as the first four-week session: lay flat on the bed, Plexiglas lowered, lead blocks strategically placed and radiation emitted.

After four weeks had passed, I was relieved to be finished with the radiation treatments. I experienced only mild short-term side effects. These included tiredness, a suntan appearance in the radiated area and a loss of hair above the nape of the neck. The short-term side effects, although minor and manageable at the moment, would prove to be more serious years down the line. For now, I believed that my health issues had settled.

I could now focus my time, energy and efforts on home life and teaching. It was mid-November 1987. I looked forward to returning to a 'normal' home and school routine. I was feeling very good. Especially as a first-time teacher, I was currently better able to focus on my students by preparing lesson plans and executing these plans in the classroom with more energy. I was even able to contribute to school life by helping with extracurricular activities such as coaching track and field and helping to run our school's fashion show and prom.

Life was returning to a new but more consistent routine, a routine that didn't involve the constant thought of cancer. This was enlightening, and I embraced it. How quickly I let myself get back into the daily rigours of life and the frequent worries of things that should not have mattered.

Hodgkin Lymphoma Recurrence

It was early spring 1988. I would be awakened fairly often at night by a sharp pain in my left leg. I would jump out of bed, walk around and try to massage the pain away. The pain would subside only to return randomly on another night. On one of those nights in particular, I felt a node in the left groin area, a node that I had not noticed before. Beyond the pain, panic set in.

Apprehensively, Dan and I returned to the cancer clinic so that I could have the lymph node looked at. I was carefully examined, and several tests were ordered. Based on the examination and prescribed tests, the radiologist needed to confirm the findings with certainty. The only way to know for sure was to biopsy the node.

I did not have pleasant memories of my first lymph node removal, so I was not looking forward to this procedure. However, I knew that I needed to get this node removed so that we fully knew what we were dealing with. I was booked several weeks later, in mid-June, for the removal of the lymph node. By this time, my first school year was coming to an end. All things considered, I felt that I had a successful inaugural year. Strangely, however, who could have anticipated that the year would be flanked by two lymph node biopsies?

This lymph node removal experience could not have been more different than my first. The calming and caring nature of this surgeon made for a much more palatable experience. Again, I was awake, and fully aware of what was going on. However this time, the surgeon froze the area, and he gently and carefully removed the enlarged node. I did not feel any tearing, tugging or pulling, nor did I feel any blood trickling down. He also kept checking with me to see if I was doing alright. He continued to reassure me throughout the procedure. How important it was to feel that I was being treated as a person.

In those times, it did not take long to get pathology results back. Within a few days, Dan and I received the news that, deep down inside, we suspected. It was the same Hodgkin Lymphoma cell type that I was diagnosed with one year prior. That new finding meant that I was now considered to be in Stage 3 Hodgkin Lymphoma due to the presence of additional cancerous cells in the groin area. See Figure 1. As you may recall, when I underwent the staging laparotomy the previous year, we knew that the results we received at that time would be 95% accurate. However, because it was impossible to test every lymph node, there remained approximately a 5% chance that random cancerous cells would still be present. Unfortunately, I fell in that 5% range.

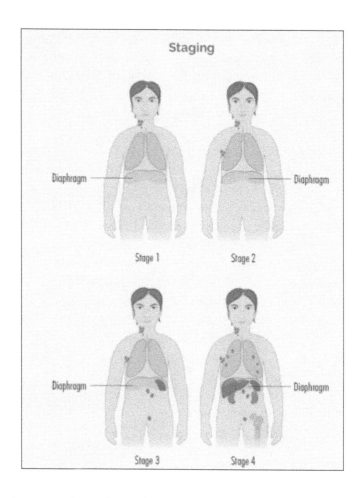

stage 1   one lymph node area is affected, either above or below your diaphragm.

stage 2   two or more lymph node areas are affected on the same side of your diaphragm.

stage 3   at least one lymph node area above and at least one lymph node area below your diaphragm are affected.

stage 4   lymphoma is in multiple lymph nodes and has spread to other parts of your body (e.g., bones, lungs, liver).

Figure 1. Staging Hodgkin Lymphoma. From Lymphoma Australia.Retrieved from https://www.lymphoma.org.au/types-of-lymphoma/hodgkin-lymphoma. Copyright (2022) by Lymphoma Australia.

Recommended Treatment

I would be returning to the Windsor Cancer Clinic once again. Dan and I had an appointment at the clinic, but this time, it would be with the chemotherapy oncologists.

Dan and I had a thorough consultation with the very first kind oncologist that we met upon first being diagnosed. She reassured us that despite the recurrence of Hodgkin's disease, the studies showed that the five-year survival rate decreased from the original 90% but still stood at about 80%. We felt encouraged by those statistics. She proceeded to explain that, at this point, there was no other option other than undergoing a regimen of chemotherapy.

As previously stated, when I was first diagnosed one year ago, had I been older and beyond childbearing age, chemotherapy would have been the recommended course of treatment. However, I was now 26 years of age. Dan and I did not have any children and freezing eggs was still not an option. We knew that the chances of conceiving after completing chemotherapy treatments stood at 50%, and for me, that was the most concerning part of the prescribed treatment.

The oncologist proceeded to explain in detail the course of treatment that I would be undergoing. She also asked if I would be interested in participating in a study for the Medical Society on chemotherapy regimens for Hodgkin's disease. The study involved using the current regimen of eight drugs versus eliminating the last drug and using a regimen of seven drugs. The research was believed to show that removing the last drug would have very close to the same effect on the overall treatment plan, but with reduced side effects.

Dan and I both agreed that it would be a good idea to be a participant in this study as I would be closely monitored throughout the chemotherapy sessions and, in addition, for several years following the completion of treatment. It would involve a combination of seven or eight drugs, and I would be randomly selected for one of the two research groups. I met with the nurse who handled the paperwork and managed the participants of this study. She thoroughly explained the study, and then after making a phone call, she informed me that I would be receiving the seven-drug regimen.

The treatment plan would take place over four-week cycles. I would receive four drugs (two intravenously and two in pill form) in week one and three in week two (two intravenously and one in pill form). I would then be off for the next two weeks, and then the next four-week cycle would begin again. The regimen would continue for another seven cycles.

Once Dan found out about the names of the drugs that would be administered, back to the cancer clinic library he went. He gathered as much information as he could about each drug, its potential short-term and long-term side effects and the prognosis after undergoing both radiation and chemotherapy. Knowledge was power.

Dan and I also wanted a second opinion from the London Cancer Centre. After my first diagnosis, we solicited the opinion of a trusted London oncologist, Dr. Bramwell. We wanted to return to her to get her thoughts on our second diagnosis and to obtain her recommended course of treatment. Packed with all the pathology reports, chest X-rays, CT scans and other test results, we left for London and met with Dr. Bramwell. She concurred with the course of treatment that the Windsor Cancer Clinic proposed. She felt that it would be better for us to have the treatments done in Windsor for convenience, and if complications arose, I could be treated closer to home. Dan and I fully believed in Dr. Bramwell, and we accepted her advice with conviction.

By this time, the school year was drawing to a close. I disappointingly informed my department head, principal and vice principal of the cancer recurrence. Regrettably, I explained that I would apply for a one-year sick leave. They were saddened to hear of the news. My vice principal was especially determined to explore job-sharing re-sponsibilities whereby I would come in to teach when I could. When I was not feeling well, she would take on my classes (things are quite different in the current education system, and this would not be acceptable now). I briefly thought about her considerate offer.

Nonetheless, I knew myself, and that when I commit to something, I am 100% in. It would be very difficult to wake up every morning, assess my current health status and determine whether I was well enough to meet the teaching demands of the day. I knew that it would not be fair to my students, my vice principal, my colleagues and me. Therefore, the best thing for all concerned parties was that I take the year off to undergo treatments and to adequately recover so that I could begin the following school year healthy and stronger.

Chemotherapy Treatments Begin

My first four-week cycle began in late August 1988. The first week, which included four chemotherapy drugs, made me very sick for several days. The drugs would inevitably wipe me out. Essentially, in that first week, I could not do much of anything. In the second week of the four-week cycle, I was administered another three drugs. These three drugs did not make me physically sick, and I felt alright. More importantly, I sensed that I was recovering from week one. In week three, my white blood cell count would drop to dangerous levels. This was a common side effect of chemotherapy, which caused not only the destruction of cancerous cells but also healthy ones.

It would be at this critical time that, with such a low immunity system, I was most susceptible to acquiring infections. The concern with picking up an infection coupled with a very weak immune system was the challenge of fighting off the infection successfully. It was for that reason that any sign or symptom of infection would be quickly followed by an antibiotic treatment. Also, in that third week, I would feel extremely weak and shaky. Week four was my bounce-back week in which I felt more energy. I regained some strength and felt quite good overall. Then, the next four-week cycle would be set in motion all over again.

In that first cycle, namely week three, I was hospitalized for a week due to an infection. Antibiotics were immediately administered intravenously to readily fight off the infection. It was only my first of eight cycles, and I thought to myself dejectedly, "If this is the way the chemotherapy treatments will continue, then I am in for a long ride."

While in the hospital, I noticed that my hair began falling out. It wasn't difficult to notice. Throughout the day, numerous strands of hair would be found on my pyjamas and on my pillow. My sister was very helpful while I was in the hospital. Each day, she would pick up the loose strands and gently groom my thinning hair. She did it in a way that I was able to hold onto my hair until I was finally discharged. I was grateful for her efforts as I made it home with most of my hair intact.

I was not afraid of losing my hair. I had my wig ready to go. However, I was hoping that the full hair loss would take place in the privacy of my home. Thankfully, that is what occurred. When I arrived home from that hospitalization, my hair had thinned out significantly. I knew it wouldn't take much for it to fall out. Dan and my brother bore witness to one of the harsh realities of chemotherapy. As I prepared for the inevitable, they watched intently with an inquisitive set of eyes and a look of uncertainty. Gently, I began the process of brushing my hair off. After several strokes of the brush, it was all gone.

Although hair loss from the effects of chemotherapy was not uplifting, as I remarked earlier, it would not be my worst side effect. Losing my hair created some funny memories that my family and I still laugh at to this day. With the loss of hair came the use of a wig. I experienced several peculiar incidents involving my wig, but one stands out. One day, as I was baking something in the oven, I opened the oven door to check on the baking dish. I must have gotten too close to the open oven because when I closed the oven door and turned to Dan, he asked, "What is that smell and what happened to your hair?"

I quickly looked in the mirror and was stunned to see that I had lost all of my bangs! The smell was that of the wig that had been singed from the heat of the oven. Dan and I looked at each other again, and we both began to laugh. "Oops, I guess I can't get too close to heat again," I chuckled. Luckily, I had a backup wig to get me out of this predicament.

After my second four-week cycle, with much the same results as the first cycle, I quickly learned I would be a write-off in weeks one and three. It was during these weeks that my mom was a blessing, especially during the day when Dan was working in Detroit, Michigan. My mom would do many of the household tasks that I was unable to do, and she would prepare meals for Dan and me. As much as I wanted to be independent, when I was down and out, the support that my mom provided for me was invaluable.

In my second and fourth weeks of treatment, I regained strength and energy, and those weeks became my two best weeks of the four.

From the onset of treatments, my oncologist and several nurses instructed me to rest when I was weak and tired and to resume daily activities when I felt good. Therefore, I tried to take advantage of weeks two and four. In those productive weeks, Dan and I hosted our annual cousins' party, had family and friends over for the holidays, took some small trips to Toronto, and did anything we could to enjoy life as much as possible.

That year of undergoing chemotherapy treatments showed that it could be quite challenging at times. I was hospitalized another three times, twice for infections and once for a blood clot in my right arm. Not knowing exactly what to expect from the treatments, it was difficult to predict what to do in certain situations.

Take, for example, the situation of the blood clot. One morning when my right arm swelled up and it became stiff, Dan and I decided to go to the emergency department to get it checked out. It was a good thing that we did because after having some tests done, it was determined that I had a clot in the upper arm. The clot was a serious issue and needed to be dissolved immediately. The process of treating and successfully dissolving the clot resulted in a one-week hospital stay. To conclude, during the eight months of chemotherapy, Dan and I found that we had to be extra vigilant in identifying unusual developments.

Ultimately, Dan and I made it through the rigours of chemotherapy. It took perseverance to do this, and we could finally look forward to better days. Once again, we hoped to return to some normality, whatever that meant. Dan and I wanted to feel comfortable with my prognosis, and we wanted to put that past year behind us as we looked forward to a future free from major health issues.

Forging Ahead

Having Hope

That year, several things stood out in my mind that helped Dan and me overcome another of life's hurdles. Firstly, we were informed by the oncologist that the combination of radiation treatments with chemotherapy treatments presented a slightly increased risk for me to develop leukemia in the future. In addition, I could experience long-term side effects from the treatments that I underwent. We knew there were potential risk factors in the future, but at that time, we had no choice but to undergo the prescribed treatments to give us the best possible chance to beat this cancer. Again, you do what you have to do with the current information that you have available.

Secondly, from the time that I was first diagnosed, Dan and I never had an issue discussing my health issues, especially if it could help others. We didn't often bring up the topic, but if someone asked questions or was interested in gaining more information about similar health concerns, we had no problem sharing what we knew. Remember, knowledge is power. We found that talking about these issues was both healing and therapeutic, particularly if we could provide support and encouragement to others.

Thirdly, I had to learn to hold on to my independence and to keep the worries of the new diagnosis and treatments from suffocating me. Luckily, from a young age and to this day, I have been a FOMO girl (fear of missing out). I have never wanted to miss out on anything. My mom used to lightheartedly tell me, "You can't have your cake and eat it too!"

During my chemotherapy treatments, this FOMO worked in my favour. I had two weeks of the four-week cycle that I would feel good. My healthcare professionals added that whenever I felt well, "Live life as normally as possible." I did just that! I got on with my life and enjoyed myself despite what I was going through. Dan and I planned outings, visits and get-togethers in those two weeks that I felt decent. I certainly tried not to miss out on too much, and I made the most of the 'good' two weeks.

In the two weeks that I was too sick, weak or tired to do much else, I had to reshape this time in my life. I needed to redirect my activities yet still make my life engaging. Hence, I spent more time reading. I read many books, mainly biographies and autobiographies of people who persevered through life's challenges. A few of my favourites included *Life Wish* by Jill Ireland (wife of Charles Bronson). This book was Jill's inspiring story of a woman who had everything, but when she faced a serious cancer diagnosis, she fought and used every means possible to save her life.

Another insightful memoir was *Iacocca: An Autobiography* by Lee Iacocca. This book described the workings of the auto industry and Iacocca's vision and determination to revive the struggling Chrysler Corporation. These books served as a source of inspiration for me when I needed to preserve my cognitive ability and gain emotional strength.

That emotional strength was paramount when I went for my first chemotherapy treatment. Dan accompanied me to the cancer clinic. He waited apprehensively for me in the waiting room with a worried look on his face while I was called into the chemotherapy suite. Not knowing what kind of side effects I would experience and/or when I would experience these effects created feelings of nervousness and unease. Due to the uncertainty surrounding the effects of these treatments, Dan and I decided early on that for the first few months, either Dan or my mom would escort me to the cancer clinic. On this first occasion, Dan would provide the assistance and mental support I required.

During that first treatment, I was seated in the suite next to a younger gentleman. While he was getting ready for his treatment, he proceeded to talk to me about the cancer I had and what treatment I was on. I quietly stated that I was just starting my first of 16 treatments. I asked him the same question, and he responded with some relief that he was on his final treatment. I looked at him in awe. I was not jealous but happy that he had reached his last treatment milestone.

Observing my hesitant expression, he looked at me and reassuringly said, "I was sitting here many months ago and wondered if I would ever come to the end of my treatments. Before I knew it, here I was at my last treatment. Don't worry. Eventually, you will get there, too."

Although it seemed like an eternity before I would reach my last treatment, his words resonated with me.

Light at the End of the Tunnel

Fast-forward eight months, and I was now returning to the cancer clinic for my last treatment. In the chemotherapy suite, I found myself seated next to another gentleman. Coincidentally, he started chatting and he asked me what I was being treated for, and then he asked what treatment I was receiving that day. In much the same way that the young gentleman eight months earlier tried to encourage and reassure me, I repeated his words to the newest patient.

I recalled sensitively, "I was sitting here many months ago and wondered if I would ever come to the end of my treatments. Before I knew it, I had reached my last treatment. Don't worry. Eventually, you, too, will arrive at your last treatment."

So, the cycle repeated itself.

For those last few years, Dan and I faced some challenging times. However, we were surrounded by the love and support of family and many friends. These people brought light to some of our darkest days. In addition, we could not have overcome these hurdles alone. It was only possible with the care and compassion we received from countless people. These included Dr. DeRose, Dr. Girvan, Dr. Bramwell, the oncologists and the nurses at the Windsor Cancer Clinic, the nurses on the cancer floor of Metropolitan Hospital, my colleagues and school administration, and so many others, too numerous to mention. We know that we could not have done it without you.

The health issues that Dan and I encountered also made us understand how fragile life was. We were reminded that we must live life to the fullest for in a moment, it could be taken away. As Dan and I prepared to continue our life journey, we were reminded to never take things for granted and to appreciate even the smallest things in life. We rediscovered the sweet sounds of birds singing in early spring, the gold and amber leaves filling the autumn skies and the peacefulness of white, soft flakes descending for the first winter snowfall.

Lastly, those years from 1987-1989, when I was between 25 and 27 years of age, were difficult ones and formed a steep hill for us to climb. However, along the way, Dan and I found a way to carve out steps and climb that hill, one step at a time. We realized how fortunate we were to have made it over that hill. Despite that, we did not fully recognize the impact that the climb would have on the rest of our lives. That steep hill, perhaps, provided a hint of what was yet to come.

My mom and dad were an important presence throughout my health challenges. It was always heart-wrenching to break the bad news to them. However, with each new diagnosis, they would muster up the strength to support me through it.

Point Pelee National Park, Leamington, Ontario: Not only was my mom extremely supportive, but she sowed the seeds for my appreciation of the outdoors and the wonders of nature.

Chapter 3

Finally a Family

In April 1989, at 27 years of age, with great relief, I finished my last chemo treatment. My oncologist thought it was best to consent to me taking May and June off so that I could adequately recover from treatments and be healthy and ready for the start of a new school year in September. She also recommended refraining from trying to conceive for one year post-treatment to give my body time to fully rid itself of all of the toxic chemotherapy drugs consumed in the last eight months.

For me personally, my greatest concern about undergoing chemotherapy treatments was not about mortality or losing my hair. It was more about infertility and the real possibility that I would not be able to bear children. As stated earlier, the clinical studies at the time showed a 50% success rate of being able to do so. During those eight months of chemotherapy, I did not menstruate, nor did I resume even eight months following treatments. How could I even think about getting pregnant?

According to the Canadian Cancer Society, it should be noted that:

> Chemotherapy drugs can stop the ovaries from working properly and releasing eggs (ovulation). The damaged ovaries and loss of healthy eggs can lead to treatment-induced menopause. This may be temporary or permanent and depends on many things, especially your age. (Canadian Cancer Society, October 2020)

This is when we were referred to an Obstetrician/Gynecologist who dealt with infertility, Dr. Greg Hasen. Dr. Hasen was very empathetic and caring regarding our situation. He understood my strong desire to start a family. Dan was very supportive of my desire, but he also reassured me that no matter what happened, he would be content and accepting of what was meant to be.

After undergoing several tests, Dr. Hasen prescribed a drug to stimulate ovulation. I was given a three-month prescription. In months one and two, nothing happened. In the third month, my period resumed only to cease the following month. Dr. Hasen informed me that this could well happen, so I was not surprised. However, I began feeling different and unlike myself. I did not think I could be pregnant, but my symptoms would lead me to believe otherwise.

Pregnancy Test

Hesitantly, I took a pregnancy test all alone, and I anxiously waited for a result. As I remained still, my heart started beating quickly and my hands trembled. I anxiously shifted my gaze to the test, and my eyes widened. I was shocked and in disbelief when I saw that the test showed a positive result!

I waited for Dan to return home from a baseball game he had played that afternoon to share the news. With a bewildered look on my face, Dan turned to me with suspicion. I could not hold back, and cautiously gave him my newly found information. The news came like a bolt from the blue. Suspicion soon turned to skepticism then turned to pure joy. Initially, he did not believe me until I showed him the proof. To say that Dan and I were both relieved and ecstatic was an understatement!

My pregnancy went well, and I was able to teach throughout it. My due date was December 1, 1990, and toward the end of October, when I went for my monthly checkup with an obstetrician from Dr. Hasen's team, he noticed that my blood pressure had increased to serious levels. He immediately advised me that I would be admitted to the hospital. He then gave me strict orders that I was to be on bed rest until the time that I was ready to go into labour. Anxious thoughts raced through my mind – good health, smooth pregnancy, now high blood pressure? I wondered what was happening, but I knew I had to take care of this baby at all costs.

For the next week and a half, the baby and my blood pressure were both closely monitored by Dr. Hasen. He weighed the cost of delivering the baby too early and the benefit of not allowing high blood pressure to affect the baby. After a long and tenuous ten-day bed rest, in the early hours of November 6, 1990, three and a half weeks prior to my due date, my water broke. A short time later, Dr. Hasen entered my room for his early morning visit. With a smirk, he stated reassuringly, "Well, we certainly don't have to wonder what to do anymore."

I immediately called Dan, who was already on his way to work in Michigan, and I excitedly explained to him that the time had arrived. Dan reached the hospital shortly after, and I was whisked off to the birthing room with him in tow. After a fair amount of time in labour, I was finally ready to give birth. At 2:16 p.m., our beautiful baby girl was born! We named her Jenna Danielle. Dan and I were beside ourselves and could not contain our excitement and pride over our miracle baby. In our hearts Dan and I truly believed that that's who Jenna was – our miracle.

Over the next few years, Dan and I shared many fulfilling moments and heartwarming experiences with our daughter, Jenna. I often think back to the positive energy she exuded and continues to do so. From a young age, I had her accompany me to the Canadian Cancer Society's Daffodil Drive to raise money for cancer. Each year, Jenna and I would be part of a larger contingent who sold bunches of daffodils at our local shopping malls and grocery stores. With her bubbly personality, lively actions and curly ponytail bobbing up and down, she would excitedly ask shoppers if they wanted to purchase daffodils. Thankfully, our crusade was profitable as the shoppers had a tough time refusing. In short, Jenna brought immense joy to our lives and Dan and I embraced our roles as mommy and daddy.

Unexpected Outcome

The fall of 1992 had arrived, and Dan and I were ready to expand our family. Again, conceiving became a challenge, and it was rec-ommended that we seek out the assistance of a renowned fertility specialist in the London, Ontario, area. Following a consultation and after undergoing several tests, we were seated back in his office to hear the dismal news. We were informed that we most likely would never be able to have any more children. We were told that we were very lucky to have our daughter and that we should feel very fortunate to have one child, as many couples could not have any. As true as that statement was, receiving the upsetting news greatly saddened Dan, primarily because he knew the impact that it would have on me. For me, I was shattered.

Dan, always looking at the glass half full, accepted the news with positivity and optimism. On the positive side, he was grateful that we were able to have a child, our daughter, Jenna. He was also very optimistic that we could enjoy a fulfilling life with our family of three. I, on the other hand, was left heartbroken with the new diagnosis.

Once some much-needed time passed and I was better able to digest the infertility news, I gained a clearer picture of our situation. After sorting things out in my head, I knew that I was grateful for the one child we were able to have. Even so, with Dan's support, we were not quite ready to give up. Once again, we returned to Dr. Hasen, our local obstetrician/gynecologist, for further advice and a second opinion.

When it was our time to meet with Dr. Hasen, he reviewed my health records and the test results from the fertility clinic in London. He shook his head, and with furrowed brows, he remained skeptical of the news that Dan and I received. He felt quite optimistic that we had a chance of conceiving again. Dr. Hasen then decided to prescribe the original drug that I took to kick-start my first pregnancy. He would give it three attempts, and if that drug did not work by the third try, he would then prescribe a second fertility drug that would further stimulate ovulation. Although Dan and I did not want to get our hopes up, at least we felt we had a fighting chance.

Much to our disappointment, Dan and I experienced three unsuccessful attempts using the original drug. With that, Dr. Hasen advised us on the common practice of taking some time away from fertility treatments altogether. However, he remained committed to trying the more potent drug after taking a break from treatments.

Once that healing period had elapsed, Dr. Hasen was ready to start on the more aggressive fertility drug. Again, it would involve three separate attempts. This time, on the first try, Dan and I waited and hoped. Disappointedly, we experienced no success. After trying the newer drug for the second time, we were disheartened to learn that, once again, nothing happened. We knew that if we were not successful on the third trial, it would mean moving on to the next stage of fertility treatments. Dan and I began the process with that third trial, and waited and hoped.

A Positive Test

The wait for the third trial of infertility treatments was finally over. The third attempt ultimately proved to be a successful one. Imagine how elated we were when Dan and I found out that we were pregnant for the second time! We found luck at last on our third try. Jenna was thrilled with the prospect that she would be a big sister. Dan and I were simply overjoyed to be parents again!

During this second pregnancy, I never wanted to know the sex of the baby as I looked forward to the element of surprise. Although Dan probably would have wanted to find out, he obliged. Once again, my pregnancy was a good one, and I could continue my teaching duties throughout it. However, the main difference between my first and second pregnancies was that from early on, the baby moved around a great deal more than Jenna ever did. As mentioned earlier, this was ironic because, from a young age, Jenna was an energetic and active girl with a larger-than-life personality, nothing like she was before birth! Nonetheless, I was fortunate to have two sound pregnancies.

The months of the second pregnancy passed without incident. During that time, I felt so well that I could even assist in coaching our Senior Girls' Basketball team. As I was entering my ninth month of pregnancy, I was starting weekly checkups with Dr. Hasen. With less than a few weeks until my due date, I visited Dr. Hasen for my first weekly checkup.

At that visit, Dr. Hasen checked the baby's heartbeat, and it was good. He then examined me, took my blood pressure and took measurements. He proceeded to inform me that I was ready to have this baby very soon and that I probably would not make it to the weekend! I remember that it was a Tuesday. Excitedly, when I returned home that day, I wondered whether I should go to work the next day. Dan and I gave it some thought. Because the baby and I appeared to be doing well, Dan and I decided that the best thing to do was to go into work on Wednesday. This would help in keeping me busy and distract me from what lay ahead.

I went to work the next day and experienced a good and uneventful day at school, all the while anxiously awaiting the birth of our second child. Later that evening, after arriving home, Dan was scheduled to play basketball in his adult league. He debated about going, but I insisted, reassuring him that I would be fine.

Our Second Child

While Dan was at his basketball game, it dawned on me that I could not remember the last time I had felt the baby. Caught up in my school tasks and responsibilities during the day, I thought back and could not recall feeling the baby move. Given that this baby was significantly active from early on in my pregnancy, it was out of the ordinary for me to be experiencing this. I sat there quietly and waited for some movement. There was nothing. When Dan returned home, I shared my concerns with him. Not wanting to overreact, he suggested that we just try to relax, watch, feel and wait for any movement. Once again, there was nothing. After waiting an hour to witness some movement, to no avail, we decided to go to the hospital to have things checked out.

A range of emotions came over me. I felt uncertain, in disbelief and confused, yet I had a glimmer of hope. I wondered, "Could this be happening?"

We entered the emergency department and explained to the triage nurse what we were experiencing. Without delay, she sent us to the obstetrics floor.

On the obstetrics floor, the nurse quickly set me up to the heart monitor. Wand in hand and gel spread over my belly, she searched, and we listened for a heartbeat. We did not hear a sound. Not giving up, the nurse proceeded to get another heart monitor explaining that sometimes the monitors could be faulty. When she left the room, Dan held my hand. Deep down inside, we could sense the outcome. I could not even make eye contact with Dan, knowing I would break down if I did. I did not have to look – I could just feel his sadness. Our worst fears were coming true.

In no time, the resolute nurse returned with a new monitor. She repeated the process, spread more gel over my belly and started scanning with her wand. She searched, and we waited. We listened. Again, there was no sound. We could not hear the thumping of a heartbeat. We knew we had lost our baby. Our baby's fate had been sealed.

Heartbroken and devastated yet shocked and speechless, we wrestled with our thoughts. As the nurse gently picked up her instruments and packed up the equipment, she quietly left the room. We had our private time to begin making sense of the inexplicable.

In the wee hours of the morning, Dr. Hasen was called to inform him of the situation. He arrived at the hospital a short time later, around 1 a.m. The doctor entered the birthing room with sombre eyes, and his head lowered. In his characteristic empathetic way, he showed deep regret and was truly apologetic. It was not his fault, though. I was then given some labour-inducing drugs. Reassuringly, Dr. Hasen told us that he would not be far away while waiting for me to go into labour.

As promised, several hours later, Dr. Hasen returned to the birthing room when I was ready to deliver our baby. The delivery happened in the early hours of January 13, 1994, coincidently, on Dan's mother's birthday. The delivery was quick, it was quiet, and when all was said and done, our solemn selves laid eyes on our full-term beautiful baby boy. There were no sounds, no crying, no joyful shouts, nothing. There was just our baby boy, Jordan Michael, born still.

The nurses gently took Jordan away for a short time to clean him up. They soon returned with our little guy, cleaned and bundled up, wearing a cute knit cap on his head. Dan and I carefully held him, our tears rolling down, and with a heavy sigh, our heads dropped. Amidst the quiet, we could faintly hear a song playing in the background. We made it out. It was the song from Eric Clapton, *Tears in Heaven*, a song Clapton had written after the untimely death of his young son.

The stillbirth of our son, Jordan, was a particularly tough pill to swallow. He was born at 3:48 a.m., and we left the hospital the following day. From the hospital, Dan and I returned home that day to a neatly made empty crib. There were no cries or signs of a newborn baby, just quietness and stillness. Our three-year-old Jenna, who was staying with my parents, kept asking, "Why couldn't we take this baby home?" We did not have answers. We only had questions, mixed feelings and emotions, immense sadness, resentment and overall emptiness.

Coming to terms with losing Jordan and the whole grieving process proved to be a challenging hurdle to overcome. Whereas everyone around us went about their lives, and rightfully so, our world had stopped. No one ever got to know Jordan, so for an outsider, he did not even exist, but to Dan and me, he was the son we lost. He was the son we never got to know, the plans left unfulfilled, and the dreams we would never realize.

They say time heals, and that is a true statement in my mind. Dan and I worked through our grief, recovery and healing, but we certainly never forgot Jordan. As well, we gradually came to terms with our loss and adjusted to life without him. It was important for Dan and me to begin to move forward, especially for our daughter's sake.

A Big Scare

Three months after we lost Jordan, I remained off of work on maternity leave. I was scheduled for a routine CT scan for the Hodgkin Lymphoma study I was a part of. As you may recall, the study compared the patient survival rates of those who had eight chemotherapy drugs versus those who had seven chemotherapy drugs. It had been seven years since I was first diagnosed with the disease. I was now going for CT scans twice a year, a change from the original four times yearly. These were regular CT scans that decreased in frequency as time passed, but were still necessary to stay on top of any abnormal developments.

A few days after having the scan done, I received a call from the cancer clinic. I thought this was odd, especially because it was the oncologist who had called. However, I listened with some concern. He told me they had found a large mass behind the stomach area. I stopped dead in my tracks. No one ever wants to hear the words 'a large mass' found anywhere in your body. My heart sank, my legs weakened, and my voice went shallow. All of a sudden, I felt paralyzed. Through the shock, I tried to make out the rest of what the oncologist was explaining. I deciphered that I would be required to return to the hospital to have the mass biopsied. I hung up the phone, shook my head and felt sheer emptiness. Dan and I were faced with yet another hurdle to overcome, but this time, the hurdle seemed insurmountable.

Not long after receiving that troubling call, I would be booked one week later for another CT scan to precisely locate the mass. The scan would then be immediately followed by a needle biopsy. The biopsy was a procedure whereby cells from the mass would be extracted through a needle and tested. That week was one of the longest weeks of our lives, and Dan and I feared the worst. I would find myself walking around the house with my head in the clouds, focused mainly on the thought of this large mass. I spent a great deal of time with Dan and our daughter, worrying about how much time I would have left with them.

The long week finally passed, and nervously, Dan and I found us back at the hospital. Dan sat patiently in the waiting area as I was accompanied to the CT scan room to be prepared for the procedure. The technologist operating the CT machine scanned my abdomen area once and then scanned it in reverse. This process was repeated several times. I could hear talking in the background, but I could not make out what was being said. Again, the action was repeated, and more discussion occurred. The next thing I knew, I was moved out of the scanning field.

The nurse came to my side and began removing tape around the intravenous site. Puzzled but still nervous about the situation, I wondered what was going on. While she removed the intravenous that contained a contrasting dye, she reassuringly said, "No needle biopsy needed today!"

At this point, completely baffled, I asked her to repeat what she had just said.

She said the same words again only this time she added, "No needle biopsy needed today. We compared your current scan to that of the previous week. The radiologist determined that the large mass was a shadow."

I could not believe my ears. I shook my head in disbelief. I felt the weight of the world lift away. How relieved I was and how relieved Dan would be! When Dan and I met outside in the waiting area, our eyes welled up, and we hugged each other. It is difficult to accurately describe the moment, but suffice it to say, we felt on top of the world! We knew that we had narrowly escaped a grim diagnosis. We were now ready to move on in life.

Another Try

It was the summer of 1994, and we were six months removed from the loss of Jordan. This period brought forth a desire to have another child and hope that I could conceive one last time. We would always remember Jordan, as he would forever be our guardian angel. However, we wanted another brother or sister for Jenna and I, in particular, wanted to have another child. Our obstetrician, Dr. Hasen, had moved out of town. But before leaving, he recommended his partner, who also specialized in infertility, and assured Dan and me that we would be in good hands.

Dan and I had a consultation with the new obstetrician. His plan was very similar to that of Dr. Hasen's. He was going to prescribe the more aggressive fertility drug that I had been previously prescribed prior to the second pregnancy. His plan also was to give it a maximum of three tries. If we did not conceive after the third time, then the doctor would begin fertility injections to improve the chances of pregnancy.

After failing to respond to the drug therapy following the planned three attempts, I began to undergo the injection therapy treatment. Again, this therapy would involve a maximum of three trials. If I did not respond by the third attempt, the next step would be to go through a process called intrauterine fertilization, in which sperm are medically placed into the uterus. Dan and I were hopeful to avoid a more invasive procedure, but willing to go there if needed.

Unexpectedly, on the third attempt of the injection therapy treatment, Dan and I found out the news that we were long awaiting. We were pregnant once again! In each of our experiences with fertility treatments, the third time was a charm! As fortune would have it, after being given a 50% chance of conceiving following chemotherapy treatments, we were able to do so three times.

My third pregnancy went smoothly, and I felt good throughout, much like I had experienced with the other two pregnancies. However, because of what occurred at the end of the second pregnancy, I was being closely and more frequently monitored, not that it was a factor in losing Jordan. Throughout the pregnancy, Dan reminded me to try and not get over anxious, but I must admit that what happened with Jordan always remained in the back of my mind. I was due at the end of July 1995. My obstetrician indicated that he did not want to take any risk, and he did not want me going to full-term. For that reason, he scheduled me to come into the hospital on July 21 to be induced.

In the early hours of July 21, we left Jenna with my mom and dad while Dan and I left for the hospital. After being induced and following a relatively short labour, at 10:20 a.m., our adorable son, Justin, was born. His middle name was going to be Jordan, a reminder that Justin would always have a part of his big brother with him. I am not sure if it was just in our heads, but the resemblance of Justin to Jordan warmed our hearts. We were simply over the moon with the successful induction and safe delivery of our beautiful and healthy baby boy, Justin Jordan!

Later that morning, my mom and dad brought Jenna to the hospital to meet her little brother. Dan and I thought we were overjoyed and excited with our new son, but that was an understatement. When Jenna met her little brother for the first time, the sparkle in her eyes and the bounce in her step said it all! She came up to me and whispered in my ear. Tearfully, I answered, "Yes, Jenna, we can take this baby home!"

In 1995, pictured here on Justin's Baptism Day are my dad and mom, me, proud big sister Jenna, Justin, Dan and Dan's mom, Virginia. Our guardian angel, Jordan, can be spotted in the foreground.

Forging Ahead

Have Hope

Knowing that following chemotherapy treatments, I would have a fifty-fifty chance of having children gave rise to worry and concern in my life. Despite this, it brought signs of hope. Dan knew how important this was to me, so he fully supported my efforts. However, Dan would have been content regardless of how things worked out, children or no children. Family and friends around my age were getting pregnant. I will be honest that it was difficult to witness. On the one hand I was very happy for them, but on the other hand, I longed to have my own child. Hope got me through those trying times. Dan and I did not know how things would work out, but as long as there was some chance, we were always hopeful for positive results.

In regard to my fertility issues, there were some difficult times that Dan and I faced, and we frequently found ourselves in uncertain situations. I was 28 years old prior to my first pregnancy and at times, I would be asked when we were planning to start a family. The ironic part was that we were planning to start a family, and we were trying. People meant well, but they did not realize the impact of their well-intended questions. During these taxing times, it made me further realize how important it was to be sensitive to others. It was certainly important to choose our words carefully, as we did not know that others could be suffering in silence.

Facing our fertility challenges, it was important for Dan and me to have a doctor who we could connect with, someone who was understanding, compassionate and supportive. That is exactly what we found in Dr. Hasen. From the moment we met him, he was someone we could develop a relationship of confidence and trust. He listened to our concerns, he understood where we were coming from, and he did not give up on us. He gave us much-needed hope, encouragement and guidance through the journey ahead.

Furthermore, and most importantly, when we knew that we had lost our baby at full-term, Dr. Hasen immediately came to the hospital in the middle of the night to take care of his patient. He remained close by, ready to deliver the baby when I went into labour.

You cannot get through these moments on your own. He was there for us in some of our most difficult times. We could not have been more impressed by Dr. Hasen's steadfast support and personalized patient care.

It was extremely hard to lose Jordan. It was made even more difficult by the fact that he was a full-term baby and that I had no issues at any time throughout the pregnancy. I carried Jordan longer than I carried either Jenna or Justin. Yet, after losing Jordan, Dan and I found comfort in believing that we would always have our guardian angel looking over us. He would appear unannounced as the red cardinal perched on the evergreen in our backyard. We would spot a duckling waddling through our lawn, following mother duck to the water and we knew it was a sign of him. Jordan would appear to us in many ways, oftentimes helping us through some of our most trying times.

A few months after Dan and I lost Jordan and after receiving that fateful call from the cancer clinic, we anticipated the worst. Following the misdiagnosis, Dan and I felt a renewed lease on life. We were re-minded again of how fragile life can be and how we have to remember to take nothing for granted. I remember reading, 'Learn to appreciate what you have before it's no longer yours to appreciate.'

Set Priorities

Finally, and particularly after the birth of Justin, Dan and I wanted to take advantage of every opportunity we could to spend quality time with our family. By then, Dan had left his information technology position in Michigan with General Motors and Electronic Data Systems. The commute to various locations in Michigan was becoming longer and more onerous and he found himself spending an increasing amount of time on the road. It was a major decision in our lives, but one that Dan felt compelled to make.

Just prior to Dan leaving Electronic Data Systems, he decided to pursue a career in teaching and thus to become a high school computer science and math teacher. He had set his priorities in place. Dan knew that realigning those priorities would allow him to enhance our family life, precisely what he was looking for.

Dan and I always believed that the best learning for our children took place through life experiences rather than material things. One of those experiences was exploring Canada. We wanted our children to learn more about and discover our country. So, in the summer of 2000, we travelled to the west coast of Canada. By this time, Jenna was nine and Justin was four, and we wanted to take them to Alberta and British Columbia. What made this a particularly special trip was that my mother and father accompanied us on this venture, a trip they had long dreamed of.

In the summer of 2000, my family travelled to western Canada with my mom and dad. Here we are with my cousin, Dana, inside the famous Hollow Tree in Stanley Park, Vancouver, B.C.

Uncovering the beauty of Canada's west coast was awe-inspiring. The stunning contrast between the majestic mountains of the Rockies and the iconic lakes of the national parks was unmatched. Dan and I would plan day excursions to soak in all this natural beauty. We would pack a picnic lunch of freshly baked bread, sweets, tasty deli meats and European cheeses. After a morning of driving by landscapes resembling postcards and visiting scenic sites, we would take a break. We would unpack and enjoy our goodies while we embraced the scenery surrounding us. This also gave Jenna and Justin a chance to run around and wear off some energy. After a well-needed stop, the six of us would continue our breathtaking trek.

Along our scenic drives, we would be eager and thrilled to discover wildlife such as mountain goats, caribou and moose. In one instance, we spotted a bear close to the roadside. Excitedly, we slowed down the car and pulled over to the side of the road to get a better look. All of a sudden, my dad quickly got out of the car. Not knowing what the bear could do, I shouted to my dad, "Get back in the car."

My dad stayed put. I shouted again. He did not move. On the third attempt, I yelled, "Dad, shut the door!"

With that command, my dad finally shut the door. The only thing though, was that he shut the door, leaving himself on the outside. He stubbornly misunderstood the point. After a few heart-pounding seconds, my dad made it back into the vehicle.

Having journeyed through Canada's western provinces two years prior, in the summer of 2002, we wanted to tackle the eastern parts of Canada, including Quebec, New Brunswick, Nova Scotia and P.E.I. This was a long road trip and Jenna and Justin were 11 and 6 years old at the time. This was prior to iPads, cell phones or modern car conveniences. Without the latest technology, they needed to be creative in keeping themselves engaged during these lengthy car rides. Relying on a DVD player and music helped Jenna and Justin pass the time. Jenna once joked, "How do you think I learned the words to all the Backstreet Boys' songs?"

When we arrived in New Brunswick, I wanted to take the family to see a place called Hopewell Rocks. This was home to the world's highest tides found in the Bay of Fundy. In the morning, the tides were so low that the Atlantic Ocean floor exposed huge, sculpted sea stacks. By evening, the tides had risen so high that the ocean floor was completely covered, and now smaller sea stacks appeared to be floating on water. Although we were amazed to walk on the ocean floor during low tide that morning, we barely made it back to witness the evening tide phenomenon.

We narrowly missed the spectacle because I wanted to make the most of our time in New Brunswick. I did not want to waste the six hours between low and high tide. Excitedly, we left Hopewell Rocks that morning to explore New Brunswick's protected wilderness and pristine beaches. Leisurely enjoying one of those beaches in the late afternoon, I soon realized we were a long distance from our starting point. We were going to miss the high tide scene that we had purposely planned. We quickly gathered our belongings and packed up the kids. We anxiously headed back to Hopewell Rocks, hoping to return before the park gates closed. Driving down snaking roads, around lush forests and along salmon-filled rivers, we finally arrived at dusk just in time to experience the striking landscape and the marvel of high tide!

The Canadian adventures were amazing, but our family was fortunate enough to also travel to many of the U.S. states. We admired the incomparable erosion of the Grand Canyon and felt the enormity of the California redwood trees. We heard the shouts of fish vendors at Seattle's Pike Place Market, embraced the Atlanta Olympics and savoured the Cajun cuisine in the French Quarter of New Orleans. These gifts for the senses were not only instrumental in educating us as parents, but they were also key in stimulating and inspiring our children to discover their future adventures.

It was important to note that meaningful life experiences did not have to involve big trips around the world. Some of our family's most memorable times were a short distance from our home. Those moments could have been packing up a picnic and enjoying it in one of our favourite parks, going for bike rides to our waterfront, or simply walking the trails in our community of Southwood Lakes. Oftentimes, it was the simple things in life that brought us the most happiness.

One of those simpler things was to take Jenna and Justin to the park to read to them one of their favourite Harry Potter books. We would walk a block to a platform hanging over the small lake in our subdivision. The platform was an eight-sided wooden structure that we fittingly termed 'The Octagon.' There we sat and as I read, they listened intently. When we got too tired, I closed the book, and we left The Octagon for home. It seemed so simple. It was such an easy thing, but it was a worthwhile one that Jenna and Justin remember fondly. Regardless of the scale of the experience, the key takeaway was to embrace the moment before life took a turn.

Chapter 4

More Hurdles to Overcome

Don't Sweat the Small Stuff

It was 2005, and life was good. While in the recent past, we were balancing our fears and hopes, it was comforting to feel that those trying times were behind us. At 44, my life had returned to a more consistent and regular routine. There were fewer medical tests to take or doctors' appointments to attend. The children were growing up, they were busy in school and actively involved in their sports. Dan and I were preoccupied with our teaching and coaching. It seemed like so long ago that we had faced our challenges. We were now ready to move on.

Consequently, the further removed I was from my health issues, the easier it was to lose sight of where I had been. It was human nature, I suppose. The intense emotions of worry, fear, despair and hope released in the past were now fading with my recoveries. Family responsibilities such as cooking and cleaning and ensuring that the kids were ready for school and their activities became our priorities once again. I soon discovered that I was getting caught up in the daily grind of life.

Take, for example, a typical after-workday. It might have included planning lessons for the next day, photocopying handouts and completing paperwork. Then, I would head to my school gym to meet up with Dan to watch Jenna's volleyball match. After the match, the three of us would return home. Dan and I would prepare dinner while Jenna and Justin worked on their homework. We would then tidy up from dinner, help Justin with his Grade 5 homework and prompt him to get ready for bed. Fifteen-year-old Jenna was independent and capable of taking care of herself. Finally, I could mark assignments and complete the following day's lessons. If time allowed, I would watch some TV before bedtime. After a well-needed sleep, the sequence would continue the next day.

Sound familiar? Something you could relate to? This was no different than what most other families experienced. Yes, it was often stressful, but I felt these situations were family stressors that we assumed as parents in everyday life.

It was the self-imposed stressors that restricted me from seeing the bigger picture. For instance, preparing a dish for a special dinner and it not turning out quite the way I would have wanted caused me stress. Slight digs or jabs that people made caused me tension. I found that I was worrying too much about trying to make things so perfect, or I was over thinking what people said or thought. Essentially, as we often find ourselves doing, I was sweating the small stuff.

Then suddenly, I was stopped in my tracks. I was unexpectedly faced with more health challenges. One of those issues surfaced while Dan and I went for a walk one day. Out of the blue, as I walked, I lost control, and my body began veering to the left. Without warning, I was unable to walk straight. It did not last long, and I was able to complete the walk without incident, but it left us dumbfounded as to what had caused this. Then a few weeks later, while I was having a conversation with Dan, my speech became slurred and I was unable to get my words out properly. Again, this was short-lived. Nonetheless, it was concerning enough that our family doctor referred me to a neurologist.

During the consultation with the neurologist, he had me complete a series of clinical tests. Upon a thorough observation, he was certain that I did not have Multiple Sclerosis. Despite that, he ordered an MRI of the brain to rule out MS and to determine what had caused those incidents a short time earlier. It was reassuring to learn that the MRI confirmed that I did not have MS. However, it did show signs of Transient Ischemic Attacks or TIAs otherwise known as mini-strokes. A new revelation emerged that would be added to my medical history. This would leave me with yet more health uncertainties and another thing to be concerned with.

Despite this, given that the two independent incidents were short-lived and isolated, it was determined that no further intervention was immediately required. I was to have a follow-up appointment with the neurologist. In the meantime, if I experienced further symptoms, I would proceed to the nearest emergency department. To some extent, relieved by the news, Dan and I remained cautious, but were again reminded that we could not take anything for granted.

Risky Hypertension

Seven years prior to these mini-stroke incidents, in 1998, I was diagnosed with hypertension or high blood pressure. During that time, my blood pressure was very erratic. I was not overly concerned about this because I always thought it could be controlled. Contrary to that, it turned out that it was not so straightforward. Controlling the high blood pressure proved to be quite challenging. Consequently, if left untreated, it could cause serious health concerns for me in the future.

To control the high blood pressure, my family doctor put me on a particular drug. It would work for awhile, and then my blood pressure would increase or decrease to dangerous levels. My readings reached as high as 196/116 or as low as 66/44. This occurred quite a few times in those seven years. After trying several different drugs with no consistent success, it became necessary to go to the next step. Thus, my family doctor wanted to refer me to an internist, a specialist who dealt with high blood pressure issues. Once again, we sought the help of our trusted friend, Dr. DeRose, to point us in the right direction. Dr. DeRose recommended seeing the reputable Dr. George Dresser at the London Health Sciences Centre in London.

In July 2005, during the initial consultation with Dr. Dresser, Dan and I found him to be another very adept and compassionate doctor. He listened closely as we explained my medical history and our concerns. As we updated him on the list of blood pressure medications that I had been taking in the past, we could tell he was intent on helping us to solve this problem. After undergoing a series of heart tests, Dr. Dresser prescribed a different blood pressure drug, one that I had not been previously prescribed. The hope was that my blood pressure readings would improve.

For the next ten years, from 2005 to 2015, my blood pressure continued to be problematic as it fluctuated between significant highs and dangerous lows. We would regularly see Dr. Dresser, and he would adjust the dosage. In several cases, he would put me on a different blood pressure drug altogether. All along, Dan and I noticed Dr. Dresser's critical thinking skills hard at work trying to solve the extreme volatility of my blood pressure.

In addition, on one of those visits, when Dr. Dresser checked my heart, he found that I not only had a heart murmur, but he detected a concerning sound. The sound led him to believe that several of my heart valves were leaking. Somewhat worried and concerned, Dan and I listened closely. The doctor indicated that in time this condition would result in restricted blood flow throughout the body. This would in turn, cause serious health ailments. Therefore, the condition would require regular monitoring for the time being. Eventually, I would need surgery to rectify the problem. Little did Dan and I know at the time how severe this situation would become.

Within that ten-year span, in August 2011, I experienced a distressing event. It was August 8, and I received a call from my mother. She said that she was bringing my father to the emergency department as he uncharacteristically stopped mowing the lawn due to extreme weakness and fatigue. Without blinking an eye, I said I would meet her at the hospital.

When I arrived at the hospital, my mom and dad were waiting patiently in the ER room. Blood work and several other tests had been ordered, and my father, my mother and I now waited for results. In the early hours of the following day, we received some alarming news. We presumed that my dad had something that would explain his severe weakness and tiredness. However, we did not expect this. My mother and I were blown away when we learned that my father had an acute form of leukemia, a rare and aggressive cancer that affects the blood.

My heart sank. My throat tightened. I suspected that my mother was experiencing similar feelings. She and I did not immediately turn to face each other as we did not want to break down. We kept our eyes glued on the doctor to gather further information. Occasionally, my mother and I glanced at my father to see how he was doing. We took a quick peek to observe his facial expression. We did not want him to take note of our stunned looks, and by now, our eyes were welling up. So, we tried to keep focused on the doctor. We wondered whether my father understood the diagnosis or the seriousness of the situation. By his sombre look, my mother and I guessed he knew it was not good.

My father was immediately admitted to the hospital. Early the next morning, my father, mother and I met with the oncologist handling my father's case. When the kind, empathetic oncologist met with the three of us, she explained that my father had a very aggressive form of leukemia. More importantly, she added that this specific type of leukemia had not responded well to traditional treatments. The news left us solemn, deeply saddened and desperate. The three of us knew that my father was facing an uphill battle.

The oncologist continued to inform us that although my father's chances of survival were low, there was a current clinical trial going on for his type of leukemia. It involved a unique combination of chemotherapy drugs that met with a small degree of success but would be quite difficult to tolerate. My father listened to the information presented. Without hesitation and with a glimmer of hope, he responded, "I will give it a try."

Alongside my father's undeniable will, our family would help and support him in his fight. This involved around-the-clock care provided by our family. I usually took the morning routine to meet with the oncologist, gather updates on my father's health status and ask pertinent questions. I would end my shift by getting him a Tim Horton's coffee with the usual single cream and half a sugar. My mother's role was to accompany my father to any tests, phone relatives to update them on his situation and provide overall moral support.

My sister took care of my father's care. She made sure that his hair was groomed, and his face was shaved. She moisturized his skin, gave him massages and ensured that his pillow and linens were clean and comfortable. My brother handled the technical aspect. He brought in a larger TV, FaceTimed my father's relatives in Italy and spent quality time with my father simply reminiscing. Essentially, my father was very content in his private hospital room, and the family endeavoured to make it look and feel like home.

Over the next two weeks, my father battled through the difficult chemotherapy treatments. My family looked on despairingly, desperate for any sign of hope. Further tests were completed at that time only to confirm that, unfortunately, the leukemia was not responding to the treatments. It was progressing at a startling rate. My father did everything that he could, and he fought hard through it all. His determination and will to survive were palpable. Despite that, when my family realized there was nothing else that could be done for him, each one of us came to terms with his fate. One month after his diagnosis, on September 10, 2011, sadly, my father passed away.

In 2012, shortly after my dad passed away, we attended the Transition to Betterness Event in honour of my dad. Pictured here are Dan, me, Michael, my mom, Cindy and my brother-in-law, Raffaele.

Bone Loss

The grief and emotional strain of my father's diagnosis, illness and ultimately his passing resulted in a very stressful time in my life. The buildup of unsettling events in such a short period of time took a toll on my health, particularly on maintaining a stable blood pressure. Not surprisingly, my hypertension was adversely affected and became a more serious problem. Even with my prescribed medication, it was difficult to control the extremely high readings that I was experiencing. With an ensuing visit to Dr. Dresser and a minor change in medication, the belief was that following this traumatic period, my blood pressure levels would slowly return to acceptable levels. Only time would tell.

Six months after the passing of my father, in the spring of 2012, I was disheartened to find out that I had osteopenia. This is a condition whereby there is a decrease in bone mass, causing bone weakness. It was not surprising to learn of this diagnosis since part of my chemotherapy treatments for Hodgkin Lymphoma included the drug Prednisone. A common side effect of using the drug Prednisone was the progression of bone weakening. Due to this diagnosis, I would have a bone mineral density test yearly to measure the amount of bone mass. Although osteopenia was not considered a disease, it was a warning that my bones were losing strength.

Two years later, by 2014, the osteopenia had unfortunately developed into full-blown osteoporosis. Disheartened to hear this discouraging news, I quickly realized that I would now be at greater risk for spinal problems and bone fractures. I felt dejected that I had another health issue to be aware of, to contend with and to effectively manage. Nonetheless, it was at this time that I began bi-yearly injections of the drug Prolia to slow down the bone deterioration process. Osteoporosis is often called a silent disease due to the lack of symptoms until a bone is broken. Luckily, I was made aware at the onset that I had the disease, so I could begin to take necessary precautionary measures.

Forging Ahead

Smell the Roses

Demanding work commitments and hectic daily living responsibilities translated to a busy life. This was commonplace. The key was maintaining a healthy work-life balance and prioritizing what was important in our family's lives. I needed to remind myself. Stop. Look around. Think back.

Keeping this in mind, Dan and I knew that we wanted to keep our priorities in check. We were assured of the current moment, but we were not guaranteed anything beyond the present. Facing my latest health concerns between 2005 and 2014 solidified our belief that we had to make the most of each moment. Except for the hurdles I encountered in those nine years, I was feeling good overall. Dan and I, and our children, wanted to take advantage of those times of good health. We wished to continue our aspirations to see the world.

You could often make excuses or declare that it was not the right time to take a trip, but Dan and I made travel a priority. So, we planned a family trip to Europe in the summer of 2006. The itinerary included stops in London, Paris and several cities and towns in Italy. We chose Italy because it was important that Jenna and Justin learn about and better understand their heritage. We wanted our children to discover the birthplaces of their grandparents and to explore the areas where their grandparents grew up.

To undertake this discovery, we first visited the southern region in Italy known as Calabria, where Dan's parents were born. When we arrived in the small town of Sant' Ippolito, we were amused by the older ladies peering around the curtains of their doorways with cynical looks on their faces. They were doubtful of the strangers who were walking along their cobbled streets. Everyone knew everyone in the town. Clearly, the ladies did not know us. They communicated amongst themselves and, in their Calabrian dialect, questioned, "But who are these people?" Our family was charmed by the welcome we received in that quaint southern town.

Our travels then took us to the northern Veneto region of Italy, where my parents were born and raised until their teenage years. My proud father took us to his original farmhouse and then to the farmland that had been recently developed to house his relatives. He was excited to take the family to the 'mercato' in town, where he used to purchase fresh meat and local produce such as radicchio and persimmons. My father's delight and pride in showcasing his childhood days were difficult to be outdone.

Nonetheless, my mother was equally proud to show us her city and birthplace home. Remaining was an uninhabited and unkempt dwelling located on a now busy thoroughfare. She brought our family to the walled city of Treviso, Veneto, and excitedly showed us 'Scuola dei Amicis,' the school she loved to attend. My mother then led us to the famous 'piazza' within the city walls, where she would hang out. There, we saw the 'Palace of Three Hundred.' Stark photos hanging on those palace walls brought back sombre memories of the bombing of Treviso during WWII. Despite this, the entire travel experience reinforced in me the immense pride that both of my parents had of their homeland.

The memories we made on that impressive journey remain etched in the minds of our entire family. We certainly gained an improved understanding of our heritage, culture and ethnicity. The fact that we could share this exploration with our children and my parents held a special meaning. The trip was a vivid reminder that when there is something that you want to see and do in life (and you are able), do not wait.

A Silver Celebration

It was 2009, and Dan and I were celebrating 25 years of marriage. I was doing well and whenever times were good in our lives, we tried to take advantage and make the most of those good times. Recognizing our desire to travel, we planned a Mediterranean Cruise with Jenna and Justin. The cruise took us to Spain, France, Greece, Croatia and Italy. It was a meaningful trip made even more special because Dan and I shared our 25th Anniversary with our children.

Our family treasured the memories that we held from that trip. Conversely, not all of the memories were pleasant ones. Take, for example, our first day of the trip when we arrived in Barcelona, Spain. I was eager and excited to take the family to see the 'Sagrada Familia.' As we neared the site of the well-known basilica and as I looked down at my map, I took a misstep and stumbled over a curb. My ankle suffered immediate harm. The ankle swelled up quickly, and I could barely walk. Distraught, I thought I had ruined the family trip. Almost immobile, the four of us took a taxi back to the cruise ship. X-rays were taken onboard the ship to see what damage I had done. As luck would have it, no serious injury was sustained. Alas, after purchasing my souvenir from Barcelona, an ankle brace, I was cleared to continue our family travels!

Another unnerving moment occurred when our ship was docked near Florence in Tuscany, Italy. At that port, Dan rented a car to take the family for a one-hour drive through a hidden Tuscan paradise to a city near Cinque Terre. We would take a ferry across the 'Gulf of Poets' in Liguria, Italy, to pick up a mini cruise boat that sailed to the five charming seaside villages of Cinque Terre.

When we arrived at the last of the five villages, we stopped to eat and rest at the beach. As we enjoyed the warm sun and the bright blue waters of the Ligurian Sea, I suddenly realized something. We would not make it back in time to catch the last ferry crossing the gulf! That meant we would miss the cruise ship setting sail for the next port of call. Immediately, Dan, the kids, and I packed up all our belongings and fretfully headed back to the dock to catch the first of two boats. As you may recall, this sounded uncomfortably similar to our New Brunswick adventure that happened a few years earlier.

We made it in time for the mini cruise that again passed by the five villages, but as expected, we missed the ferry traversing the gulf. Panicked, we desperately wondered how we were going to cross the gulf and complete the one-hour drive back to board the cruise in time before it set sail. We nervously looked around, and at a nearby kiosk, we anxiously asked for options.

Fortunately, a private speedboat owner witnessed our dire need. He offered to take us across the gulf for a minimal cost to retrieve our rental car. Left with no other option, the four of us boarded the speedboat. Totally unexpected, the speedboat was an exhilarating, fun-filled ride and became a lasting memory for the whole family. We arrived at our rental car and trekked the one-hour car ride along the Tuscan roads to finally return to the cruise ship in the nick of time. True to our word, Dan and I continued to fulfill our goal to live life to the fullest!

In Cinque Terre, if not for this private boat owner, we would have never made it back to the ship on time before it set sail again. This boat ride ended up being one of the highlights of that trip.

Jenna and Justin are pictured here with Dan and me
on our trip to the Mayan Riviera in 2012.

No Regrets

Building memories was very important to Dan and me. When our
daughter Jenna embarked on a one-year supply teaching venture to
Australia, we hoped that, along with Justin, we would be able to
visit Jenna and travel Australia's eastern coast together. That hope
became a reality in December 2013, four and a half years after we
travelled to Europe. Dan, Justin and I flew to the land down under.
As we travelled the Great Ocean Road, hiked to Australia's eastern
tip and snorkeled in the Great Barrier Reef, I had to pinch myself as
I could not believe I was living these moments.

One memory that stands out is of our catamaran journey to the
Great Barrier Reef on Christmas Day. As we submerged ourselves
in the Coral Sea to snorkel in the reef, Jenna and Justin took hold of

my hands. Together, they guided me to incredible surprises. We glided toward the neon blue tang "Dory" fish, the fascinating marine life and ultimately the incredible sea turtles. To this day, that underwater adventure, in which I was literally and figuratively connected with the kids remains engraved in my mind. When I reflect on that entire trip, I know that we had created memories that would probably never occur again, but that would last a lifetime.

My family visited Jenna in Australia. You can't miss the iconic Sydney Opera House in the background.

Seizing the moment while your loved ones are still living is key. As I mentioned earlier, after only a month of being diagnosed, my father passed away peacefully at 78 years of age. He was hospitalized for the duration of his illness. Fortunately, there was time for my family to share our fondest memories with my father, to say our final goodbyes and to let my father know how much we loved him.

My family knew full well that there would be no time left to experience other events or to make future memories with my father. Hence, my family, including my mother, my sister and my brother, took comfort in knowing that we seized the special moments in my father's life while he was alive. The quality time spent in family gatherings and the memorable trips that my father took with my mother and with each of his children and grandchildren provided solace to us, albeit in a difficult time. We did not wait for tomorrow to build memories and to share quality time with my father. For that reason, we could have no regrets.

Soon after my father's passing when I was diagnosed with osteoporosis, Dan and I gathered a great deal of information to make us more knowledgeable about the disease. If there was anything I could do to slow down the deterioration of bone in my body, I would try to do it. We learned that exercise and diet were vital to treating osteoporosis. In terms of exercise, we knew that bones get stronger if we strengthen our muscles. Therefore, I needed to incorporate a daily workout regimen of weight-bearing exercises to strengthen my muscles and ultimately to strengthen my bones.

Regarding diet, eating foods and using vitamins to promote good bone health would help to deal with my osteoporosis. This meant that I needed calcium and Vitamin D-enriched foods in my diet, such as dairy, fatty fish, green leafy vegetables and nuts. To sum up, healthy lifestyle choices were not only important to help me manage my osteoporosis, but they would become crucial in helping me battle the health challenges that lay ahead.

Chapter 5

A Baffling Bleed

In mid-December of 2016, I was busy both teaching and, like most everyone else, hectically preparing for the holidays. One morning, I woke up with little energy and not feeling very well. Despite that, I mustered up some strength to get myself ready, and I proceeded to get myself to school. I seldom took time away from work, and I felt that this would be another time that I could make it in for the day to fulfill my teaching duties. As the hours passed at school, I felt that I was getting weaker and just not feeling like my regular self. Finally, I was relieved to reach the end of my school day so that I could return home.

When I arrived home, I laid down to rest. Although, when I got up, I felt extremely lightheaded and queasy. Before I knew it, I had come around, and Dan was on the phone talking with a 911 dispatcher. He was explaining to her what had just happened. I had fainted. We did not know the exact reason for my fainting, but regardless, the dispatcher indicated that an ambulance was on its way.

Reluctant to have an ambulance called and not wanting any extra attention, I was relieved to learn that the paramedics would be arriving at the house without using sirens. When the paramedics arrived, they found that my blood pressure had dropped drastically and that my heart rate had risen significantly. I would be taken to the hospital to have further testing done to determine the cause of the fainting.

I was transported to our nearest hospital's emergency department, where I experienced another two fainting incidents. A thorough blood work assessment was completed, and it showed an extremely low red blood cell or hemoglobin count. It was determined that I was experiencing an internal bleed. Almost immediately, I received two units of blood in the emergency department, and I was readily admitted into the hospital.

Finding the Cause

On the following day, while in the hospital, I was prepared for a gastroscopy, a test to check the throat, esophagus and stomach. Thus, I could not eat or drink anything except for small sips of water. In the end, the gastroscopy could not even take place that day, and I was rescheduled for later the next day. Fasting was necessary for yet another day making it close to three days that I had had nothing to eat or drink.

Finally, the day arrived for the gastroscopy to take place. However, going into that procedure, I was left feeling very weak, lethargic and with little to no energy. Dan, Justin and my mom were present to see me off and to wish me well. Caringly, the three of them gave me words of encouragement. Not only was I unable to respond with a gesture, but I was unable to get any words out. Too frail and weary to do or say anything, the procedure could not be done soon enough, I thought.

The procedure was successful and I awoke from it without incident. Sometime later, when Dan and I received the results, as much as I had hoped, we had no definitive answers as to where the internal bleeding originated. This left me both disheartened and per-plexed. Following several more blood transfusions, my red blood cell count had gradually increased to reasonable levels. This was a positive sign. Leaving nothing more that could be done for me, after spending three long nights in the hospital, I was discharged.

Over the next few days, I recovered at home, but during that time, I started feeling weak again, and I became quite pale. I was sent for further blood work at a public lab. After having completed the blood test, Dan and I left the lab. We soon found ourselves outside on a cold December day. There was quite a bit of snow on the ground. As I slowly began to navigate the snow-covered sidewalk, my legs felt heavy and unstable. All of a sudden, my legs couldn't hold me up any longer, and I felt as if I was ready to faint again.

Dan gently placed me on a snowbank. He looked around and spotted a man approaching us. Dan kindly but hurriedly asked the man if he could wait with me while Dan went to get the car. Confused, the man complied and waited with me as Dan rushed off to retrieve the car. Fortunately, Dan returned in no time. The man walked away with a bewildered look on his face, wondering what he had just experienced. Luckily, I hobbled to the car without fainting.

Still feeling weak, Dan managed to get me home. The blood work I completed earlier in the day showed a significant decrease in my red blood cell count. I was continuing to bleed internally. Left with no choice, I returned to the emergency department on December 22. By this time, I was experiencing head rushes and, not surprisingly, feelings of weakness and fainting. In the emergency department, I received another two units of blood prior to being readmitted to the hospital for further testing.

The internist who was overseeing my case indicated that this time around, I would be undergoing both a gastroscopy and a colonoscopy. Once again, there would be no eating or drinking to properly prepare for the procedures. It had now been five days since I was unable to eat or drink since the internal bleeding began. I was extremely weak at this point. When I was wheeled off for my procedure, I could not even lift my hand to wave goodbye to Dan and Justin.

By this time, Justin was in nursing school. As a result, he was interested in knowing and learning more about the lab work and the various tests that I had done thus far. Additionally, he was curious about the tests I would be undergoing shortly. Thus, with his newly acquired knowledge, he accompanied Dan and me to many of my appointments and procedures. He would ask relevant questions, and make key inquiries. He would come to play an integral role in helping Dan and me to understand and navigate many of my diagnoses. He was becoming an advocate for my health causes.

Interestingly, studies have shown that a significant reason why students enroll in nursing is because a friend or family member has been affected by health challenges. Justin found himself in a similar situation, and that became a key factor in his decision to enter the nursing field. I learned that my experiences were the subject of many of his nursing school papers. Unknowingly, my health issues impacted the course of Justin's career aspirations.

I was transferred back to the recovery room following the successful completion of yet a second procedure to get to the bottom of the internal bleeding. Once again, after meeting with our internist, he concluded that neither the gastroscopy nor the colonoscopy provided any further definitive answers regarding the cause of the bleeding. The internist did request for me to have another test done, but he first wanted me to gain some strength and wanted my condition to stabilize. By this time, my red blood cell count had continued to increase to an acceptable level. It was now December 23, 2016, and I would be kept in the hospital for the foreseeable future.

The next day, on Christmas Eve, we waited to see if I would undergo the required test. Noting that it was Christmas Eve, we knew the chances of that happening were slim. Moreover, we knew that it would be highly unlikely that this test would take place over the next two days, namely Christmas Day and Boxing Day. I was completely disheartened to eventually learn that the area where the test was to be performed was closed for the holidays. Even though Dan and the kids would be spending Christmas with me in the hospital, I felt dejected at the thought that we would be unable to spend the holidays with our extended families.

In the late afternoon, I was feeling down and out. My nurse contacted the internist to explain that the testing would not be available until after the holidays. In that conversation, she must have advocated for my doctor to discharge me. I am not sure exactly what transpired. All I knew was that following the call, my nurse came into my room. With a smile, she indicated that my internist gave consent for me to be discharged. The permission was given on the condition that I return the day after Christmas for the test to be administered. I was thrilled! For the time being, I was able to leave the hospital to celebrate Christmas with our families! My wheels started spinning. I thought, "What must I do to get myself ready?"

Concerned that I would be spending Christmas in the hospital, my family and I were relieved to learn that I would be discharged in the late afternoon on Christmas Eve.

My FOMO (fear of missing out) kicked into high gear. Although weak and lacking energy from a prolonged hospital stay, adrenaline must have kicked in. Enthusiastically, Dan and I packed up my belongings, and we left the hospital. We hurried home to get ready. Before we knew it, we were on the road with our children, driving to our niece's home. We were about to share our traditional Christmas Eve celebration with my husband's family.

Further to our Christmas Eve festivities, on Christmas day, we shared a special Christmas dinner at Cindy and my brother-in-law Raffaele's home. We exchanged thoughts of gratitude. In my eyes, I had plenty to be grateful for – I was discharged from the hospital, I was starting to feel better, and I was with family. It is difficult for outsiders to fully appreciate what being present in these events with each of our families meant to me. All I can say was that my heart was full.

A Lost Cause

After the Christmas holidays had passed, I returned to the hospital to take the final test. Except finding out that I had a constricted esophagus, the test results provided no further evidence as to the cause of the internal bleeding. By this time, it appeared that the bleeding had subsided and that my red blood cell count was continually increasing. Despite this, to get to the root cause of the bleeding, another procedure would be necessary. Our internist informed us that the optimal way to view the digestive tract would be to undergo a capsule endoscopy.

Dan and I wholeheartedly accepted the recommendation of undergoing the capsule endoscopy if it could better help us determine the source of the bleeding. This procedure would be done in London. It involved swallowing a capsule with a camera inside to obtain a better view of the digestive system. Thousands of pictures would be taken. The pictures would be sent to a recorder that I would wear on a belt secured around my waist. It was amazing how far modern medicine had come!

In March 2017, three months after I experienced internal bleeding, Dan and I drove to London so that I could go through with the capsule endoscopy. In the hospital, after some preparatory work, I swallowed the magic capsule. In the next seven hours, we left the hospital, and we were able to move about freely. We walked around the city and went for lunch while the capsule travelled through the digestive tract. We returned to the hospital, and once the capsule fully made its way through the tract, the recorder was removed, and the results were then processed.

Several weeks later, we returned to London to meet with the internist and to receive the results of the testing. Once again, we were hopeful, but were left discouraged. Even with the more detailed and thorough capsule endoscopy, the source of the bleed could not be determined. It was concluded that the bleed had resolved itself and that no further treatment was required unless there was a recurrence. As a precaution, I would continue to have regular blood work done for the foreseeable future to test hemoglobin and iron levels. Dan and I remained baffled as to what had caused the internal bleeding issue in the first place. Nevertheless, we were thankful and hopeful that the problem had seemingly rectified itself.

Forging Ahead

Perseverance

Looking back to Christmas Eve 2016, when I was hospitalized for internal bleeding, I was reminded how quickly life could change. That day, while lying in my hospital bed, Dan and I reflected on our past, and looked toward our future. On a more immediate note, we also thought about how we were going to spend our Christmas Eve and Day in the hospital with our children. It had been a very unsettling hospital stay, and I was not looking forward to spending the holidays there.

The unsettling experience included sharing a hospital room with a woman who continually called out for help morning and night. One night, I was awakened by her shouts. She was extremely agitated, and several nurses came to the room to settle her down. The curtains were drawn shut, so I could not see what was happening, nor did I want to. I stayed quiet and tried to fall asleep with no success. At one point, the woman must have gotten aggressive. I heard one of the nurses yell abruptly, "Don't hit me!"

My eyes opened wide, and my heart began pounding. "Could she come after me?" I thought in my weakened state.

By now, there were additional staff members who entered the room to restrain her and diffuse the situation. After a significant timeframe, the staff was able to settle her down. The whole ordeal was disturbing at a time when I felt so sick myself. The incident left me startled and quite troubled.

My time in the hospital had been difficult to endure, considering the procedure preparations with no food or drink, the many invasive tests and the unruly roommate. Even though Dan, Jenna and Justin were going to spend the holidays together with me, I still felt both dejected and discouraged. Little did I know then how a very similar situation would emerge several years later. Thankfully, for now, I was able to leave the hospital and go home for the holidays.

Gratitude

I have heard that the more you are grateful for people and things, the more you have to be grateful for. In the past year, I had many things to be thankful for. For one, I was able to have blood transfusions that helped to build up my iron and hemoglobin levels. Who could imagine that one would think about being grateful for this? However, when those transfusions served to boost my energy levels and improve my quality of life, you became very thankful.

Being grateful does not necessarily mean it must be for something big. Spending those nights in the hospital made me realize how much I appreciated sleeping in my bed. After arriving home from those hospital stays, I could not tell you how thankful I was to be able to lay my head down on my pillow and fall asleep in my bed. To this day, I frequently give thanks for this small but relevant occurrence in my daily life.

To determine the cause of my internal bleeding, I underwent several procedures and tests, including a more detailed capsule endoscopy. I admit that it was frustrating to learn that after all those diagnostics, there was no conclusive evidence as to the cause of the bleeding. At the same time, Dan and I were very thankful for mainly two reasons. Firstly, we were grateful that nothing serious showed up in that thorough testing. Secondly, we breathed a sigh of relief that after several months, it appeared that the internal bleeding had resolved itself. We realized that our situation could have been so much worse and for this, we thanked our lucky stars.

There were many additional things to be grateful for. In March 2016, during our school's break, Dan and I travelled to Alberta to see our daughter. Jenna had been working for a year and a half as a high school teacher in Whitecourt, Alberta, a small town located two hours northwest of Edmonton. Jenna was completing her second year of teaching there, and Dan and I thought it would be worthwhile to visit and spend time with her.

We flew to Alberta, and spent quality time with Jenna and her boyfriend, Cameron. It was heartening to see Jenna in her western Canadian setting. Our travels gave us an opportunity to explore the snow-covered Rockies, hike scenic trails, skate on Lake Louise and frequent trendy eateries and quaint cafes. Soaking up that natural alpine beauty alongside Jenna and Cameron truly provided me with many moments of thankfulness. It has been said that gratitude generates happiness, and we could not have been more content to spend this time with special people in such striking surroundings.

Completing the Tunnel Mountain hike in Banff, Alberta, Canada, rewarded me with this stunning view.

I found that showing gratitude was very beneficial in helping me to work through my health issues. That display of thanks shifted negative thoughts into more positive ones. Some time ago, I learned that while expressing gratitude, there is no time for negative thoughts. As I faced more health concerns, being grateful for what I had or where I was became that much more meaningful. For this reason, every night before falling asleep, I began selecting three things that I was grateful for that day. Sometimes, they were big things, such as successfully making it through two consecutive endoscopic procedures, and sometimes, they were simply the smaller things in life, such as being able to sleep in my bed.

Celebrating Thanksgiving with my mom, Cindy and Michael, we knew that we had so much to be thankful for.

In the summer of 2017, I felt that retirement was getting closer. To be honest, after experiencing the latest internal bleeding issue, I began thinking more seriously about my future. I contemplated when would be the right time to turn the page on my teaching career and progress to the next phase of my life. In the past year, after experiencing several fainting episodes, after being hospitalized for a week and after undergoing some rigorous tests, I considered whether it was time to move on.

Chapter 6

An Unhealthy Heart

In January 2017, during a checkup with my internist, Dr. Dresser, he found that my blood pressure was fairly stable, and therefore, he decided to keep me on my current medication. Even so, he confirmed that the valve regurgitation or leaking of the valves was becoming more prominent. Luckily, at that time, I was not experiencing symptoms such as shortness of breath or swelling of the ankles. Otherwise, surgery would need to be done in the near future.

Dr. Dresser decided that the time had arrived to refer me to a cardiologist, one who he knew was a specialist in this area. Dr. Dresser felt confident that this cardiologist would understand when it would be the right time to take care of the valve regurgitation. Hence, he referred me to Dr. Gerard Shoemaker, Division of Cardiology and Associate Professor of Medicine at Western University, London, Ontario.

Cardiovascular Disease

Five months later, in June, I had an echocardiogram done, and one month after that, Dan and I met Dr. Shoemaker for our first consultation. From the beginning, he displayed a mild-mannered, caring and sensitive approach. Moreover, we trusted Dr. Shoemaker, and we felt confident that he had our best interest at heart. He proceeded to explain to us that the echocardiogram showed severe leaking in at least one of the valves and that surgery was imminent.

In that visit, Dr. Shoemaker advised no travel outside the province and ordered a chest X-ray, blood work and a more specialized echocardiogram. This last test, referred to as a transesophageal echocardiogram or TEE, would get a closer look at the condition of the valves. To avoid the surgical team encountering any surprises during surgery, he also scheduled an angiogram to identify any underlying problems or blockages. Lastly, Dr. Shoemaker scheduled a consultation with an esteemed cardiac surgeon, Dr. Bob Kiaii. That consultation would allow Dan and me to meet him, gain further insight and get more details on the pending cardiac surgery.

Several weeks following the June appointment with Dr. Shoemaker, we met Dr. Kiaii. He was an extremely knowledgeable yet humble doctor. He took his time to explain the entire surgical procedure to Dan and me. He laid out the pros and cons of replacing a valve versus repairing a valve, evaluated the heart function and outlined the risk factors. Furthermore, as a result of the previous radiation treatments to the chest that I had undergone 30 years earlier, damage was done to the area. That made Dr. Kiaii concerned about heavy scarring and thickening in the arteries as well as how well the chest bones would heal after the open-heart surgery. Dr. Kiaii's concern was undoubtedly cause for our concern.

Importantly, Dr. Kiaii had grounds for his concerns as research has shown, "radiation causes fibrosis of all components of the heart and significantly increases the risk of coronary artery disease, cardiomyopathy, valvulopathy, arrhythmias, and pericardial disease." (Belzile-Dugas and Eisenberg, 2021)

Considering the complex nature of the surgery combined with my underlying health problems, Dr. Kiaii concluded that the procedure was achievable, but would pose a significant amount of risk. Understandably, Dan and I were anxious about what lay ahead. Despite our feelings, Dr. Kiaii's openness and proven track record confirmed our belief that he was the right surgeon to help us overcome this challenging process.

A few days after we consulted with Dr. Kiaii, Dan and I drove to London so that I could undergo the angiogram procedure that Dr. Shoemaker had previously scheduled. Dr. Shoemaker was not available to perform the procedure, but he left me in the competent hands of Dr. McPherson. As Dr. McPherson performed the angiogram, there was some discussion taking place, but I could not make out what was being said. Sometime later, he came to my side and tapped my shoulder. I immediately thought the tap could not be a good sign.

"Your heart is pumping well," Dr. McPherson explained. "But your right coronary artery is quite calcified, and you have a 90%

blockage in that artery," he continued. "We will need to have a further discussion with Dr. Kiaii to determine how we will proceed," he added.

Much to my disappointment, Dr. McPherson also described that there was some damage done to the heart that was consistent with an occurrence of a heart attack in the past. Even though I was not aware of any such previous incident, nor did I remember experiencing any symptoms related to a heart attack, the fact was that my heart had suffered harm.

Fortunately, Dr. Kiaii was available later that day and together with Dr. McPherson, they returned to speak with Dan and me. They both agreed that the first step would be to clear the blocked right coronary artery as soon as possible. This would involve undergoing a procedure known as angioplasty, whereby a stent would be inserted into the artery to open it up and unclog the blockage. Dr. Kiaii felt that by clearing the blockage in the artery, there remained the potential of reducing pressure on the valves. In short, it was recommended to delay the open-heart surgery, to do the angioplasty as soon as possible and to continue to closely monitor the leaking valves situation.

One week later, I was booked to have an angioplasty performed by Dr. McPherson. The nurses and specialist explained what would take place and I was then set up for the plan of action. I was awake, and as the procedure got underway, I felt some tugging and pulling of my right wrist. There was also some manipulation of the wrist with significant pressure applied before a stent was inserted into the artery. Upon the completion of the angioplasty, I was wheeled into the recovery room, and Dan and I waited for Dr. McPherson to meet with us.

A short time later, Dr. McPherson came to talk to Dan and me. He explained that the stent had been inserted into the artery successfully. He also told us that during the angioplasty procedure, he noticed that the artery had become more heavily calcified and was now 99% blocked. With that news, we were very thankful that the procedure took place when it did! Dr. McPherson discharged me that day with the promise that Dan and I would stay overnight in London in the event of any issues arising. After spending an uneventful night in London except for a sore, aching wrist, we made the familiar trek back home to Windsor.

I suppose nothing can go perfectly smoothly. Less than three days later, I noticed a small bump on the injection site. Upon touching the bump, I felt a peculiar vibration. It was a very strange feeling. After contacting Dr. McPherson to report the situation, he specified that he wanted to personally check out the strange lump. Therefore, he recommended that Dan and I return to London to have an ultrasound done on the wrist.

Once in London, the ultrasound showed that a fistula had developed. In other words, erratic blood flow resulted from an abnormal meeting of the artery and vein. This was causing the vibration sensation. The ultrasound probe was then used to apply pressure to the fistula to alter the blood flow. Time was most likely the answer to the healing process, therefore, no further treatment was needed. I was scheduled to return in two weeks for a follow-up ultrasound to confirm that the fistula had cleared up. As originally predicted, probe pressure and time were enough to cure the fistula problem.

A Cardiac Crisis

It was now mid-January 2018, and I was experiencing increased symptoms of chest discomfort, weakness and dizziness. One evening, the symptoms became so significant that Dan and I contemplated what to do. We erred on the side of caution, and Dan called an ambulance. It was never a pleasant experience to have an ambulance come to your home with its lights flashing, to be assessed by paramedics and finally, to be transported to a nearby hospital. Beyond that, Dan and I just hoped the symptoms could be remedied.

In emergencies, you have little choice. After going through several tests in the emergency department, a heart attack was ruled out, as were any other serious heart conditions. That was a huge relief. However, I would be required to undergo numerous detailed tests in London to get a better picture of the condition of my heart. This would include a follow-up appointment with Dr. Shoemaker. He would assess the status of the valve regurgitation problem and ultimately determine whether it was time to perform the surgery.

Coincidentally, after 32 years of teaching and facing these current health issues, I prepared to retire in a couple of weeks. How ironic life can be at times. Similarly to how I began my career, undergoing tests and facing health unknowns, I was now ending my career with more tests and confronting more uncertainty. At that point, retirement felt so close yet so far away.

By the end of January, I had followed through with my decision to retire. At that time, my symptoms had subsided, and I felt a little better overall. Nonetheless, over the course of the next several months, I was still required to undergo further testing. These tests included a stress echocardiogram, an additional nuclear stress test and wearing a Holter monitor. They were needed to more accurately evaluate the existing heart condition.

Also, during this time, I was strongly encouraged to find a cardiologist conveniently located in Windsor to monitor my heart situation close to home. A good friend of mine highly recommended Dr. Roland Mikhail as she revealed that he took very good care of her ailing husband. I took my friend's advice. Hence, Dan and I were relieved to obtain a consultation with him. As you will see, Dr. Mikhail would come to play a critical role in my future cardiac challenges.

We met with Dr. Mikhail in August 2018, seven months after the onset of more severe symptoms. As my friend indicated, Dr. Mikhail was a caring and thorough doctor and Dan and I felt we were in very good hands with him. He also ordered some additional tests to complete the picture of my current cardiac condition. We then received all the results from the numerous tests taken. In summary, the heart appeared to be functioning satisfactorily and because I was not experiencing significant symptoms, it was determined that no intervention was needed at this time. I would continue to be closely monitored by both cardiologists, alternating appointments between Dr. Shoemaker in London and Dr. Mikhail in Windsor for every six-month checkup alongside regular cardiac testing.

Four months following the consultation with Dr. Mikhail, Dan and I started the 2019 year positively. Dan's retirement was due to occur at the end of January. By this time, I had been retired for one year. Now that we would soon be retired, we were looking forward to enjoying this next chapter in our lives together. For our retirement, we hoped to align our priorities, which collectively included tackling our travel bucket list.

In terms of my health issues, I continued to see Dr. Dresser, who stayed on top of my blood pressure situation, regulating the medication as needed. I also continued to see Dr. Shoemaker and Dr. Mikhail, who closely monitored the condition of the valve regurgitation and the heart function, along with any symptoms that I was experiencing. The satisfactory test results that I had recently received, besides being asymptomatic, precipitated the recommendation to stay the course and delay surgery for the time being.

Although my heart issues appeared to be relatively stable, for the past year, I had been experiencing difficulty swallowing. Even when eating small amounts of food and chewing them slowly, food would get stuck in my esophagus. I was referred to an ear, nose, and throat (ENT) specialist who, in turn, sent me for tests of the esophagus. The results showed that I had GERD, a more serious form of acid reflux. There was a 20% narrowing of the esophagus, again likely caused by the previous radiation treatments that I underwent. No intervention was required at the time, but the ENT specialist did indicate that if the narrowing worsened, I would need a procedure to dilate and open up the esophagus. Dan and I were relieved with the news, but especially in learning that there were no obstructions or tumours found.

The Pandemic

The new year of 2020 got off to a good start for Dan and me. Dan had been retired for a year, and I had been retired for two. My health status remained stable. Fulfilling our shared goal to travel, we booked a trip to Punta Cana, Dominican Republic for two weeks in February. It was our first time in the Dominican Republic, and we just wanted to get away to get some rest and relaxation. We experienced great weather, leisurely walks on the beach and overall, a terrific trip. We returned home toward the end of February, not knowing what the entire world was about to endure. Less than three weeks later, we faced the global phenomenon known as COVID.

Swiftly, cities were shut down, then countries were shut down and ultimately, the world came to a halt as it navigated through the dangerous effects of an unfamiliar virus. Isolation, seclusion and solitude became the new realities in our lives. However, within the healthcare system, these words were reserved mainly for infected patients and afflicted healthcare providers. The vast majority of our healthcare providers and support personnel became the critical frontline workers providing care for the most vulnerable while charting unknown waters themselves.

Having faced several health issues in the past, I must admit that I was concerned that one or more of these issues might resurface during the COVID pandemic. The last place I wanted to find myself was within the confines of a hospital, in the throes of the COVID battle. Not only was I concerned about being hospitalized, but with so many uncertainties regarding the virus, I was unsure of the effects COVID would have on my underlying health conditions. Therefore, I remained even more conscientious about isolating myself as I did not want to risk becoming infected with this mysterious virus. Fortunately, I was feeling well at the time; and I was just thankful for my current health status as it kept me away from hospitals.

Approximately five months into the pandemic, I had been lucky enough to avoid contracting COVID and to stay away from hospitals or clinics. It was now August 2020, and I was booked for a series of tests, including a routine echocardiogram in the cardiologist's office. As expected, safety protocols were in place in the office, and I felt as safe as possible considering the times we were living in. The results of the echocardiogram, however, painted an unusual picture. It showed an increase in lung pressure. With that new finding, I suspected that subsequent visits to hospitals or doctors' offices would be necessary.

Based on the lung pressure findings, Dr. Mikhail wanted to rule out lung clots, so he scheduled me for a lung scan to be completed in our local hospital. This would be my first time entering the hospital during the pandemic. By this time, the COVID surge had settled down slightly and newer and more successful treatments and medications improved overall outcomes. Despite this, I was still concerned about contracting the virus and about what effects the virus might have on me.

At the end of August, I was booked to have a lung scan done at the hospital. I do not remember many people being there, especially in the area where I was undergoing the scan. Everyone was still wearing masks, and safety precautions were being closely followed, providing me with a good sense of reassurance. I was prepared for the lung scan; the scan was taken, and once it was completed, I was asked to wait in the waiting room.

Shortly thereafter, the technologist returned to the waiting room and indicated that Dr. Mikhail wished to speak with me on the phone. Surprised that he wanted to talk with me so quickly after our last visit, I knew that the results of the lung scan could not be too good. On the phone, he proceeded to inform me that the scan showed that I had small clots in the left lung.

"Oh no, not something else," I thought to myself. He stated that he was going to immediately start me on a blood thinner. Dr. Mikhail further explained that this new medication would decrease my risk of having a stroke. Demoralized and dismayed by the scan results, I needed to convince myself to feel thankful for the findings before something more serious occurred.

With this most recent diagnosis of lung clots, I became even more concerned and careful about not getting COVID. I was not sure what effect COVID might have on my respiratory system. Due to the unknowns surrounding the virus, I felt that my symptoms could be exacerbated by the existence of these newly discovered lung clots. Not that I could prevent being afflicted with COVID, but I was certainly going to try to reduce the risk as much as possible. I became stricter with safety precautions and hence, isolation and seclusion continued to be my norm, but with even more compliance.

Forging Ahead

Seize the Moment

Through the years, Dan and I often found ourselves taking the two-hour trip from Windsor to London to address the various health issues that I faced. We never minded doing the drive because we felt we were in good hands. London Health Sciences Centre (LHSC) was an education and research facility of well-trained health professionals who dealt with many medically complex cases.

Moreover, LHSC served a large geographical area and could provide care to a much larger and more diverse patient base. Dan and I welcomed every opportunity we were given to be taken care of by the expert healthcare professionals at LHSC. We felt privileged to have access to both the enhanced facilities and the advanced testing procedures.

During many of our London ventures, Dan and I made the most of an otherwise unpleasant situation. We never missed an opportunity to check out trendy cafes and new restaurants or to treat ourselves to unique shopping experiences. Sometimes, we would pick up lunch and coffee and enjoy the peace, quiet and nature-filled landscape of Springbank and Victoria Parks in London. Between doctor appointments and medical procedures, these sidebar trips certainly gave us something to look forward to, and they served to make our London trips more enjoyable. These were some of the smaller things in life that brought us much joy.

On several occasions, Dan and I would turn our London appointments into a short excursion. On one of those trips, we booked a charming Bed and Breakfast in Bayfield, Ontario. Accompanied by my mother, we explored the shores of Lake Huron, admiring the amazing views. We enjoyed relaxing with a morning cappuccino, walking the quaint streets of small towns and capturing some beautiful sunsets.

On some other London trips for my medical appointments or procedures, Dan and I would plan a getaway to Niagara on the Lake, Ontario. The town was picturesque all year round. In the spring and summer, it was adorned with beautifully landscaped flower beds and marked with old-fashioned horse-drawn carriages. We very much valued and cherished these special moments that this dreamy town provided.

Ironically, on one such trip in the summer of 2017, while I was lying in bed, I started to feel some cardiac-related symptoms of chest pressure and rapid heartbeats. Not knowing if it was anxiety or symptoms of something more serious, I became nervous, and I tried to take deep breaths to settle things down. It was nighttime, and as I lay awake in a dark and unfamiliar place, I began thinking seriously about my health and my future. I weighed the pros and cons of continuing in my teaching career. The more I thought of it, the more I realized how short life could be, especially with the symptoms I was currently experiencing. It was at this precise moment in time that I made the firm decision to retire from teaching by the end of January 2018, a mere six months away

Live Life

The months and weeks leading up to my retirement did not pass by without their challenges. In that time, I experienced intermittent bouts of chest pressure and burning, dizziness and overall weakness. In January, with only a few weeks to go before I retired, my symptoms worsened, and I landed in the emergency department once again. I seriously wondered if firstly, I would be alright and, secondly, if I would make it to retirement. Fortunately, after undergoing several tests, it appeared that I did not have a heart attack, and my symptoms improved, so I was discharged. I would be required to undergo more in-depth testing, but for now, I still had hope that I would retire.

At long last, the end of January 2018 arrived, and I made it to retirement, finally! I can say that I was so thankful to have experienced such a fulfilling and rewarding career in teaching. In my retirement speech, I wanted to convey my feelings of gratitude and offer a message of hope especially for those facing life's adversities. An excerpt from this speech is included below:

"Six weeks after my interview for my first teaching position, I was diagnosed with Hodgkin Lymphoma. I began the first few months of my teaching career by going daily after school to the cancer clinic to undergo radiation treatments. All was good after that until the end of that first teaching year when I experienced a recurrence, forcing me to take my second year off to undergo chemotherapy treatments. I share this not to gain sympathy, but to instill a sign of hope. When I returned to teaching, and for many years after, retirement was a figment of my imagination. But as 5 years turned into 10 and 10 turned into 20, suddenly retirement became more real. And here I am now, just four days away."

My first day of retirement was met with mixed emotions. I felt proud that this momentous day was also the day that Justin began his career as an ER nurse in Detroit, Michigan. How cool was that? The last day of my career was the first day of Justin's. I also felt relieved to have finally reached this milestone. Lastly, I felt disbelief as it seemed surreal for me to have realized this specific life goal. Now, it was time to make the most of it. Living life to the fullest was a message that both Dan and I believed and lived. Dan was still teaching, but we took advantage of the school breaks to continue our travels. During March break, we took a trip to the Mayan Riviera in Mexico. Walks on the soft sand beaches, sun-filled skies and interesting readings provided the restful and relaxing setting we both wished for.

In the early months of my retirement, I underwent a number of medical tests and made visits to several doctors and specialists. Fortunately, my health status remained stable. In keeping with the theme 'living life to the fullest,' I wanted to fulfill a long-awaited goal. I had always wished to visit several European countries that I had not seen before, so for my retirement, Dan and I planned a European vacation. We selected mainly an Eastern European itinerary in the summer of 2018.

I took pleasure in researching, exploring and planning for any of our trips and this time I was preparing for our European adventure! We visited Amsterdam, Budapest, Prague, Krakow, Berlin and Munich. Exploring different cultures, eating diverse foods, visiting historical sites and admiring picturesque settings made for interesting and fun experiences. We took advantage and embraced those special moments this trip provided us with. This was my retirement reward for reaching this milestone, and I was very thankful for it!

My first year of retirement gave me a sense of freedom and more time to explore new interests. I was able to spend increased quality time with my mother, whose memory was declining and who needed more care. I was also able to focus more on my health. It is not that I neglected it prior to retirement, but I was now in a better position to eat more healthily, get more restful sleep and exercise regularly. I built a daily morning exercise regimen that included stretches to maintain healthy bones for osteoporosis and cardio to build cardiac health. I continued to follow through with my medical tests and doctors' appointments, and once again, I was thankful that my health was relatively good.

To make the most of our lives together, Dan decided to retire in January 2019, one year after my retirement. For his retirement, he selected Australia, New Zealand and Hawaii as the trip of choice. Australia always remained a unique spot for our family and one Dan and I had often desired to return to.

As I wrote earlier, Australia was where Jenna spent a year as a supply teacher and where she first introduced us to this faraway land. A few years later, Australia became home to our son, Justin. In his third year of Nursing at the University of Windsor, he decided to do a four-month exchange in Melbourne, Australia. There was no doubt that Australia held a special place in our hearts and became a preferred destination.

New Zealand was another wish list stop for Dan and me. Ever since Jenna and Justin travelled to New Zealand and returned with rave reviews, we decided that it belonged on our bucket list. In addition, Hawaii was the halfway point between Australia and Windsor, and hence, it became a suitable stop off for our trip back home. Moreover, Hawaii was where we spent our honeymoon, and we always hoped to return to those islands. In further pursuit of our life dreams, Dan and I could not wait for our much-anticipated travel explorations to these exotic destinations.

After months of research and planning, Dan and I were thankful that I was feeling well and that we would be able to embark on this terrific opportunity. Literally, a few days after Dan's retirement, we boarded our flight to Melbourne, Australia, to begin our adventure down under. We felt so fortunate to have realized this dream, and the trip was nothing short of amazing! We relived old memories from our previous Australia trip, but we also built new ones.

In Australia, we explored the Outback, hiked along oceanside trails, snorkelled in the Great Barrier Reef and enjoyed diverse cuisine and top-notch barista style coffees. New Zealand provided awe-inspiring activities, stunning scenery and the "wow" factor with every turn on the road. A New Zealand highlight was the challenging Tongariro Crossing, a 20-kilometre alpine crossing. After completing that demanding physical hike, I was proud of my accomplishment. To this day I must rank it as one of my greatest athletic feats! Hawaii topped off the experience with its spectacular landscape, dramatic coastlines and impressive beauty. Opportunities like this come once in a lifetime and Dan and I made the most of it!

Getting ready to snorkel along the Great Barrier Reef off the Australian Coast.

In 2019, in Taupo, New Zealand, I completed the 20 km Tongariro alpine crossing!

On a side note, the people of both Australia and New Zealand, especially the New Zealanders, were very health-conscious and embraced a healthy, active way of life. This offered me many opportunities to work on my health, namely, to build strength and endurance and secondly to make nutritional meal choices. I was able to maintain good physical fitness and stamina as Dan and I hiked some breathtaking trails, biked adventurous tracks and walked long distances exploring different parts of the countryside. Regarding nutrition, almost everywhere we travelled in these two countries, nutritional food options existed, and we were able to make healthy meal choices throughout our travels. The active lifestyle of both the Aussies and the Kiwis, and the nutritional and healthy food options, provided a good environment for me to live healthily.

Try Something New

As previously stated, 2020 got off to a good start, and my health remained stable. As part of my retirement gift from my children, I received a one-month membership for hot yoga, and I remembered doing it a few months after I had retired. The temperatures were high, and the sweat was pouring down. I was not too impressed, and I did not find hot yoga enjoyable.

Contrary to that, I thought I would give regular yoga a try. I was never one to go to a fitness centre or gym facility. Interestingly, I searched the Internet for workouts and stumbled upon *Yoga with Adriene (https://yogawithadriene.com)*.

My first yoga session with Adriene was part of a series, *30 Days of Yoga with Adriene.* I thought, "Wow, a challenge of daily yoga for 30 consecutive days?" Dan and I were taking a two-week vacation to Punta Cana, Dominican Republic, in the upcoming week. Could I even imagine taking on this challenge and continuing it on our trip? Why not?

Adriene's connection to the real you, along with her quiet and soothing voice were enough to get anyone hooked, beginning with me. The week before leaving for our trip, I started the 30-Day Challenge. When we arrived in Punta Cana, I continued doing yoga every morning while overlooking the dramatic backdrop. Taking the occasional peak, I would observe the turquoise waters, swaying palm trees and sunny skies. Yoga soon became one of the most mindful, therapeutic and healing practices to help me through my myriad of health issues.

I read that in retirement, one needs to try something different, and I chose yoga, hoping that it would improve my fitness level, balance and cardiac health. I had no idea that yoga would be so helpful in enhancing my resilience and strengthening my mind, body and soul. I am proud to report that the 30-Day Challenge that I began in early February 2020, has extended to year six! *Yoga with Adriene* evolved into my absolute 'must do' daily activity. It sustained me through the isolated times of COVID, the challenge of several cancer diagnoses and multiple major surgeries. Yoga enhanced my breathing and, most importantly, it relaxed my mind by allowing me to retreat from thoughts of worry and feelings of anxiousness. *Yoga with Adriene* played an integral role in improving my physical and mental well-being and shaping my outlook on life.

Calm, balance, ease, stillness and peace were meaningful words, particularly when facing health challenges. I first encountered that string of words during the first year of COVID when my son, Justin, introduced me to meditation and strongly encouraged me to begin meditating. When I first tried a few sessions, I was not fully engaged in the mental practice. However, in next to no time, I was better able to focus my mind and my breathing on the exercise. I learned that 'When you relax the mind, the body relaxes; when you relax the body, the mind relaxes.'

With the introduction of meditation, my morning exercise routine increased to include stretches, cardio, yoga and meditation. If my time was limited, I would eliminate one or two of those, but always kept up with yoga. That morning routine helped me work through many of my health battles. Meditation allowed me to think more deeply about a thought to achieve a calm and clear state of being. One such thought that resonated with me then and remains with me to this day is 'I have never met a strong person with an easy past; the present may not be easy, but it will make you stronger.'

Chapter 7

Side Effects

Suspicious Spots

I always knew that the radiation and chemotherapy treatments that I underwent in the late eighties could result in serious side effects. One of the side effects of radiation therapy was skin cancer. Sure enough, in the early 2000s a few spots presented themselves on my chest and upper back. I was referred to a dermatologist who removed the suspicious spots and he then had them tested. The results came back, and the spots were basal cell carcinoma (BCC). Basal cell carcinoma is a type of skin cancer. It is a slow spreading cancer, but if left untreated can grow deeper under the skin and could cause damage to nearby nerves and blood vessels. The fortunate news was that it was the least risky type of skin cancer and, if caught early, the prognosis was very good.

From that point forward, I would have regular appointments with the dermatologist as the likelihood of developing more skin cancer spots was high. I would also have to monitor the susceptible areas for dubious marks. At every checkup, I would report new suspect spots to the dermatologist. He would check out these spots and look for new ones himself and then determine whether the spots had the attributes of basal cell carcinoma or other skin cancers. Those spots that were deemed potentially cancerous would be removed and were then tested. Over the course of many years, I had quite a few spots removed. Without a doubt, I felt reassured that they were caught early, and no further damage was done to the surrounding tissue.

In the fall of 2020, the world remained isolated, and people were cut off from one another and from the rest of the world. It was at this time that I felt a scaly patch on the crown of my scalp. Giving it little thought, I was unconvinced that it was anything serious.

Despite this, Dan would look at the patch often and he would check for changes. It was itchy, but we hoped the itchiness would subside and that the flaky patch would go away. Over the course of the next month, neither of the two happened.

I had an upcoming routine appointment with my dermatologist. He examined the spot on the scalp, and he was curious as to how I had found it. It was located at the back of my head and my hair covered the spot. Typically, it would have been more difficult to detect. The dermatologist determined it was suspicious, and he referred me to another specialist who was more experienced and equipped in handling skin lesions of the scalp. With that, I became more uneasy and skeptical about the area in question.

I met with the second dermatologist, and he did seem to be knowledgeable and familiar with working on skin spots of the scalp. He felt quite certain that the spot was basal cell carcinoma. The dermatologist squeezed around the crown of my scalp to determine if the skin was pliable enough and whether there was enough skin available to do a skin graft. He seemed to think so. The procedure would be done in the hospital as an outpatient. The affected area of the scalp would be frozen, and no sedation would be needed. I was confident that I could weather the storm. I just hoped that the dermatologist was accurate in his initial diagnosis that it was predictably basal cell carcinoma. Then I hoped that it had not spread to other surrounding tissue.

The procedure was scheduled for December, and we were still in the midst of COVID. As mentioned earlier, I was trying to avoid the hospital setting during the uncertainties of COVID if possible, but I had little choice. I wanted to get the spot on my scalp removed as soon as possible. Unable to enter the hospital during those restrictive times, Dan dropped me off at the front doors of the building. He would be required to wait outside of the hospital. When my procedure was completed and when I was ready to be discharged, the hospital would contact Dan to let him know that I could be picked up.

Contrary to what I was hoping for, the procedure ended up being quite intense, especially at the onset. I was placed on an examination table face down on several towels. There was no massage headrest with a hole to allow for easier breathing. Instead, with my face compressed on the towel covered table, it made breathing very difficult.

In challenging times throughout my life, I relied on breathing techniques and exercises to support me. I used these breathing strategies to help me through three natural childbirths and through many of my health procedures and post-surgeries. At a time when I most needed controlled breathing for this situation, I was barely able to breathe at all without getting anxious. Fortunately, just prior to the procedure, I thought of placing my hands on the table so that my forehead could rest on my hands. Alas, I was able to breathe through a slight space between the table and my face. I could now return to my deep breathing techniques.

The affected area of the scalp was frozen and was then shaved. Similar to my first lymph node removal, I could hear and feel certain actions such as the scraping, filing and grinding on my scalp. I had to remember my breathing strategies, deep, diaphragmatic breaths in and slow, long breaths out. As I concentrated on my breathing techniques, the crusty spot was carefully removed. A flap of skin was created and flipped over the open sore. Lastly, the incision and the flap were stitched in place. Once again, thank goodness, the focus on and use of sound breathing helped me through yet another medical procedure.

The crown of my scalp was bandaged up. Due to the positioning of the excised spot, it was necessary for me to be fitted with a netted cap. The cap was placed over my entire head and holes were cut out to accommodate my eyes, nose and mouth. It was not a pretty sight, but you do what you must do to recover during the healing process. My procedure was now complete, and Dan was called to pick me up.

When I walked out of the hospital doors to meet Dan, his first thought was about how I made out with the procedure. Once I made him aware that I was alright, his second thought was what to make of the new look. I knew that he wanted to crack up, but he tried his best to maintain a serious expression, afraid to offend me. After looking in the car mirror, I realized that the best thing that we could both do was to laugh because I looked hilarious!

Two weeks following the removal of the skin spot, I returned to the dermatologist's office to receive my results. Because of my first cancer diagnosis in 1987, I tried not to take any biopsy results for granted. I was stung then and I felt once bitten twice shy. Hence, ob-taining results became a time of worry and concern for me and this time was no different. With bated breath I waited. Finally, as the doctor suspected, the spot was basal cell carcinoma. Nervousness soon turned to relief. He proceeded to show me the report from the pathologist. I read reassuringly that the margins were clear of carcinoma. It was the best news I could have hoped for.

Just as I was getting over one scalp lesion, less than six months later, in May 2021, I felt and noticed another suspicious spot on the back of the scalp closer to the nape of my neck. It had similar attributes of the spot that I had removed six months prior. It was red, itchy, flaky and after some time, it was not healing. Back to the dermatologist I went. Again, he suspected it was another case of basal cell carcinoma and indicated that it needed to be removed in the very near future.

It was now June and I returned to the hospital to have another ulcerated area on the scalp excised. Six months ago, the event left me with an unpleasant impression and I was not looking forward to repeating it. In spite of my previous procedure, I was hopeful that this time around the experience would not be nearly as daunting. For starters, when I was positioned face down on the examination bed, the nurses placed a small cushion on my forehead to keep my face elevated from the bed. This allowed me to breathe easier and to feel less claustrophobic. Secondly, the spot was smaller than the first spot that was previously removed. Thirdly, the skin was more pliable in that particular area and thus was easier to work with. I kept my fingers crossed that these three factors would make for a less traumatic experience.

The surgical procedure was repeated in much the same way as the first time around only this incision would not involve a skin grafting. The area was frozen then it was shaved. An incision was made to remove the affected area. Once the ulcer and surrounding skin were excised, the area was stitched up and bandaged.

Throughout the procedure, I maintained controlled breathing. My anxiety level was significantly reduced due to the less severe nature of this second spot removal. I was less nervous during this procedure. I was also more relieved that due to the location of the ulcerated area, I was not required to wear the netted cap as had been the case with my first experience. An elasticized gauze, resembling a hairband, was placed around my head to hold the bandaged area in place. It was a little more flattering than the original netted cap!

Dan and I again waited two weeks to receive the results from the second pathology report. We went back to the dermatologist's office and waited with anticipation. Luckily, much to our relief, the report showed that it was another case of basal cell carcinoma. Once again, the doctor had me read the portion of the report that stated that most importantly, the margins were clear. In the course of six months, I underwent two quite invasive procedures. The vital part was that both procedures turned out to be the less serious form of skin cancer and thankfully the cancers had not spread to the surrounding tissue.

Bone Density Loss

As these cases of basal cell carcinoma unfolded, my bone strength had decreased quite significantly over the years. Hence, I was referred to an endocrinologist. For the last seven years, I had been on injections called Prolia that would be administered twice every year. Prolia injections slowed down the bone deterioration process.

However, there emerged a game-changing drug on the market called Evenity. Evenity actually increased the formation of bone. In other words, whereas Prolia slowed down the bone loss process, Evenity built bone mass. The endocrinologist recommended this drug as the preferred course of action to improve my osteoporosis. It came in an injection form. Two injections would be administered monthly over the course of twelve months. Although the risk was extremely low, there was an indication that one could experience a heart attack while on this medication. Due to the state of my heart and to my overall health status, the doctor did stipulate that we would follow the Evenity regimen, but that he would observe my condition closely and proceed with caution.

I started the Evenity program and after four months, I met with my endocrinologist for a follow-up visit. He closely assessed my situation and reviewed the side effects of the injections. Again, although it was low, the risk did exist of developing more heart complications while on Evenity. Based on my medical history, he decided to suspend the medication until further notice. He felt that I would have still gained the benefit of being on this bone-building drug for four of the twelve months. In the end, the doctor did not want to risk further complications or other serious side effects and hence, took me off of Evenity.

During the skin cancer diagnoses my heart valve situation continued to be closely monitored and remained an ongoing concern. In the spring of 2021, just prior to the removal of the second scalp ulcer, I underwent several diagnostics to check the status of the heart valve leaking that I was experiencing.

It was now August, when Dan and I met with Dr. Shoemaker to go over the results of the cardiac testing completed several months earlier. As previously noted, receiving results was always a concerning time for us, especially due to the volatility of my cardiac issues. Evidently, the testing showed that the three compromised valves appeared to be relatively stable with no significant change from my previous echocardiogram. The cardiologist again recommended that because I was not experiencing serious symptoms at the time, that we should stay the course. Though we were reminded that I did have coronary artery disease and that eventually, surgery to replace and/or repair the valves would be inevitable. To put it simply, it was not a matter of if, but when the surgery would be necessary.

Forging Ahead

Being aware of changes to your body and acting on these changes early made key differences in my life. The number of basal cell carcinoma spots that I had removed, initially began with an otherwise inconspicuous mole on my back. The mole was first detected back in the early 2000s by my massage therapist. She made me aware of the spot and strongly recommended that I have it checked out. After seeing several doctors about the suspicious spot, they felt it was nothing serious. It was not until I underwent treatments for several other skin conditions that the suspicious spot was removed and tested. Sure enough, it turned out to be basal cell carcinoma (BCC). Fortunately, the early finding made by my massage therapist, together with self-detection helped me catch and successfully get treatment for the skin cancer before it spread.

Staying connected and being conscious of changes to one's body cannot be overstated. When you are given a sign or a signal, it is important to act on it. Too often people are diagnosed with cancer after it is too late because the signs were so subtle and could easily be ignored. It is not to say that self-detection is the most crucial thing in identifying illnesses early on. Regular checkups and routine diagnostic testing are also extremely important. However, self-awareness certainly does help to improve one's chances of successful outcomes and more importantly, survival.

As I mentioned earlier, to help me through challenging events, I needed to rely on what I knew from the past, essentially good breathing strategies. The removal of the suspected spot on the scalp in December 2020 became more tolerable by taking steady, deep breaths in and exhaling slowly. Controlled breathing helped me to manage my nerves and distracted me from the actual excision. Again, mindful breathing assisted me through another precarious procedure. Now that I became more active with yoga and meditation, I further recognized the benefits of breathing for my emotional state and for my overall health and well-being.

'Asian Pear,' 'Onion Bag,' 'Swim Cap,' 'Hair Net' were just a few of the terms that my family nicknamed me when I returned home from the hospital the day I had the first of two BCC spots removed from my scalp. The tightly fitted head netting with only eyes, nose and mouth exposed was a site to behold. As you know, Dan was the first to witness my new head ornament when he picked me up at the hospital. My good friend's father often would say to her, "It's better to laugh than to cry." That's exactly what Dan and I did! When I arrived home, my children greeted me as they tried to keep themselves from laughing. As much as they tried to be serious and empathetic, they could not hide their snickers. That is when the string of pet names emerged. In keeping with an optimistic and positive outlook, in that moment, it was better to laugh than to cry!

After undergoing my first skin graft and BCC excision on the scalp, I was grateful that the second procedure was not as nerve-wracking. I was also grateful that the spot to be removed was not only located in a less precarious area of the scalp, but it was smaller in size than the first lesion. Due to my experience with the first spot removal, perhaps I detected the skin irregularities of the second spot earlier. Once more, I was thankful that the second spot was caught at a time when it did not have a chance to spread. Lastly, Dan and I were very relieved and grateful that once again, the results showed that it was a further case of BCC and that the margins were clear. After experiencing numerous skin excisions over the years, it was very easy to take these results for granted. I needed to remind myself that nothing could ever be presumed.

Taking care of my body was something that I was conscientious of and something that I tried to sustain. When I learned that my bone mineral density had decreased, I realized that I had to make an improved effort to do what I could to prevent the situation from getting worse. I started with increased calcium consumption in my diet, increased weight-bearing exercises and continued with targeted stretches. In addition, I began a new treatment regimen with the drug, Evenity. Although the treatment program was short-lived due to the potentially risky side effects, I still benefited from the shortened drug regimen. Self-care was very important to my physical and mental balance not only for osteoporosis, but it would prove to be invaluable for my future, more serious health issues.

I have always believed that when life is good, we need to embrace it, we need to enjoy it, and we need to make the most of it because it may not last. It was September 2021, eighteen months following the initial onset of COVID lockdowns and restrictions. The apprehension surrounding COVID had subsided significantly, restrictions were relaxed, and the world was slowly opening up again. Life was returning to some degree of normalcy.

In addition, my health status remained stable and I was not experiencing symptoms. Dan and I felt that life was going well and that it was time to embrace it, to enjoy it and to make the most of it. After spending much of the past year and a half in varying degrees of isolation and living within limited circumstances, we decided to take our first post COVID trip to British Columbia in September 2021. We embraced our renewed freedom in Vancouver, soaking in the amazing views of the Pacific. We enjoyed the serenity of the sunrises of Tofino on Vancouver Island, and we savoured the sunsets of Kelowna. Life was good and we capitalized on it – before it was about to quickly change.

Waiting for the sun to rise in Tofino, Vancouver Island, British Columbia, proved to be a rewarding experience!

Chapter 8

A New Diagnosis

In late November 2021, after just turning 60, I was scheduled for a routine mammogram. After having the mammogram done, I was then asked to return to the clinic the following day to have the mammogram repeated. This request did not overly worry me because I had experienced a similar situation several years earlier. At that time it turned out to be just precautionary and nothing serious was found. Thus, I tried to put it in the back of my mind.

The next day I returned to have the mammogram repeated. After waiting a few minutes to ensure that the images were sufficiently clear, the technologist asked me to remain at the clinic, this time, to have an ultrasound done. Now, I became concerned, and I felt uneasy. Once the ultrasound took place and was reviewed, the technologist returned to tell me that something was not right. I was informed that a second ultrasound would be ordered. This time however, I would be required to have it done at the Breast Cancer Clinic at Windsor Regional Hospital. At that point, I got a little nervous and my level of concern increased.

Several days later, I proceeded to the Breast Cancer Clinic to have the second ultrasound completed. Once again, the ultrasound confirmed that something suspicious was showing up. I felt my anxiety and concern resurface. The only way to find out for certain about the irregularity was to biopsy the mass. Hence, I was booked for a biopsy of the suspected node that was scheduled to take place on December 20, 2021.

For the next several weeks, Dan and I faced yet another apprehensive waiting period, all the while trying to keep busy and trying to keep our minds off of the impending biopsy. It was December, and although there was plenty to do to keep ourselves busy, anxious and concerning thoughts continued to loom.

Finally, December 20 arrived. I was anxious and nervous walking into the hospital and I knew that Dan felt the same way. I was not as worried about the actual procedure as I was about what the findings would be. Luckily, my worries and fears were alleviated due to the understanding and empathetic nature of the doctor performing the biopsy. He spoke to me in a calm and reassuring way, which helped me to remain less nervous and more comfortable. He also had a sense of humour, further easing my mind. As the procedure began, he shared his hope with me that the node would pop, indicating that the node might be a cyst. To my dismay, the punctured node did not pop.

It was December 24, and due to the holidays, I knew that I would not have the results until after Christmas. Somehow, I was relieved to know that the holidays would not be adversely affected by the news we would soon receive. Moreover, Dan and I were hosting Christmas Eve dinner that year and it was a good thing that we were preoccupied with this celebration. Even though we could not hide from our worries and concern, we were distracted by our immediate thoughts that were wrapped up in the preparations for the event.

Christmas Eve and Christmas Day came and passed and three days later, I prepared myself to make that unwanted, but necessary phone call. It was a call that I wanted to shun yet I knew I could not avoid. With that, I made the call. The receptionist picked up the phone and hesitantly gave Dan and me the news. Whatever shred of hope Dan and I held onto evaporated when we received the long-anticipated results of the biopsy. We were informed that it was breast cancer. The wind was taken from my sails. My heart sank and that pit in my stomach emerged. Suddenly, I felt the effects of my lymphoma diagnosis all over again. My fear and my worry became real and it all began to sink in.

Receiving the expected news that I had breast cancer was disheartening for me, but I knew it was even more distressing for Dan. I could see it in his eyes, and I could sense it in his demeanour. Personally, I knew the feelings I was going through. However, for Dan, he was on the outside looking in and he could only surmise how I felt. Oftentimes we do not realize how much the caregiver is suffering in those difficult times. I was certain that Dan wanted to be strong for me as he had always been throughout my past health struggles. He was always strong mentally, but at the same time he was empathetic and sensitive to my needs. After taking some time to digest the bad news, he had to regain his mental strength. Dan knew that he needed to temporarily set aside the emotions and sensitivity to focus on the task at hand – supporting me through my battle with breast cancer.

The onset of our dismal news also meant that Dan and I would have to share this news with our loved ones. Breaking sad news to our family and friends was one of the most difficult and emotional parts for me. I dreaded the fact that our news would cause our closest people to feel sorrow, feel hurt and worry for me. I certainly did not want them to suffer due to my illness. It was most difficult breaking the news to my mother and to our children. Growing up, my mother would often tell me, "From the time you get pregnant, you worry about your kids." This would be another such time when she would worry about one of her children.

Revealing the news to our children would also be difficult, especially for our daughter, Jenna. It was a happy time for her, and she felt so excited for her upcoming destination wedding. Now she would worry about my health and whether I would be well enough to share this momentous occasion with her. Despite Dan and I learning many years ago that there was never a good time for disclosing bad news, we also came to realize that it never got any easier.

Even though it was difficult to convey this news, Dan and I knew that we needed to let our loved ones know soon. For now, we put aside our fears and gathered our strength and courage to personally deliver the news. As expected, our family was taken aback and was speechless to learn of the new health challenge that I would be en-countering. The reactions varied from tears to sadness and from empathy to hope. Through it all, I felt comforted by the unwavering support of my loved ones.

As I prepared to battle this newly found diagnosis, I thought back to my family history. Breast cancer was prevalent on my mother's side of the family. My maternal aunt passed away at 47 years of age from breast cancer that had metastasized to the brain. Another two maternal aunts and my maternal cousin were also diagnosed with breast cancer, but thankfully they were treated successfully for the disease. I questioned, "Was my cancer due to a genetic predisposition?

Or was it due to the radiation to the chest that I received 35 years ago?" Perhaps it was simply that according to the Canadian Cancer Society, "about one in eight women in Canada will develop breast cancer in her lifetime."(Canadian Cancer Society, May 2024) In any event, I discovered that the cause of my breast cancer could not be determined with any degree of certainty.

Once the initial biopsy results were reviewed, a treatment plan would be developed. In my specific case, with the type of breast cancer that I had, the prescribed course of treatment would have typically been to do a lumpectomy followed by radiation therapy. Initially, I felt content and at ease with this plan. However, due to the significant amount of radiation that I had already received in the past, additional radiation to the chest area may have presented further serious health problems. Hence, my radiation oncologist did not recommend any further radiation treatments. Thus, I felt settled and resolved to the next course of action – undergo a mastectomy.

A Second Surgery

In January 2022, Dan and I met with the surgeon that would be performing the mastectomy for a consultation. The surgeon was very soft spoken, patient and caring. He explained in detail the surgical procedure that would take place, and he empathetically addressed our fears and concerns.

As an aside, Dan and I received a second opinion from a well-respected oncologist at Princess Margaret Hospital in Toronto, Ontario. The oncologist felt confident that the current radiotherapy treatments available would target the cancer directly and would only affect the part of the body being treated. Considering however, the previous radiation treatments and my other medical conditions, the oncologist also supported having a mastectomy done.

Surgery to perform the mastectomy was to take place the following month on February 3, and it would be an outpatient procedure. The hospital was experiencing a resurgence of COVID cases and hence, no visitors would be allowed to go along with the patient in the waiting or recovery areas. At a time when emotional support was so valuable, I was disheartened to learn that Dan would be unable to accompany me in the hospital for the surgery.

On the early morning of surgery, Dan dropped me off at the front doors of the hospital and I proceeded to the admitting area. Firstly, I was instructed to go to Diagnostic Imaging to have sentinel nodes properly located and marked. The sentinel nodes were the first few lymph nodes where the original breast cancer would spread to and thus was an important step in the process. Further to the mastectomy, the surgeon would remove the sentinel nodes and have them tested for potentially cancerous cells. My surgery was scheduled for late in the afternoon, so I had quite a few hours to wait, contemplate and meditate in between procedures. Meanwhile, I sat alone and waited uneasily in the Diagnostic Imaging area for my procedure. Unexpectedly, someone walked into the waiting area. When I looked up, I was surprised and relieved to see that it was Dan.

Apparently, after dropping me off, Dan entered the hospital and asked if he could wait with me prior to my surgery. Thankfully for me, they granted him permission until the moment that I would be called into surgery. Having that added moral and emotional support proved to be meaningful and helped to alleviate my fears and concerns prior to surgery. Nevertheless, there remained some concerns. Firstly, I questioned, "Would my cardiac condition be adversely impacted by the anesthetic?" Secondly, I legitimately wondered, "Had the cancer spread to the lymph nodes?"

Finally, it was time for surgery. Prior to being wheeled off to the operating room, Dan kissed me goodbye and gently whispered, "I love you." My heart began to flutter, and I felt the nerves and worry set in. As calmly as I could, I said a prayer hoping that I would wake up from the procedure. I took a deep breath and told myself to hang in there as I entered the surgical room. In there, the anesthesiologist readied me to be put under.

What felt like a short time later, I awoke from the surgery dazed and weak. Although I was groggy and unsteady, I knew well enough that I had made it through the surgery. I breathed a huge sigh of relief. My prayer was answered. My caring surgeon then met up with Dan and me in the recovery room. In a compassionate way, he indicated that the surgery was successful and that a number of lymph nodes had been removed for testing. I felt some reprieve as one of my concerns had been addressed. I had made it through surgery successfully. Now the waiting game was on regarding my second concern. I needed to find out whether the lymph nodes had been infected by the cancer.

Waiting for Results

Waiting for results for many of my health procedures always proved to be quite demanding on the mind. I tried not to worry and keep calm, but there was this weight hanging persistently over my head. I knew that the news I would receive could be life altering, but I did not want to think too far ahead. The week after surgery, Dan and I returned to the surgeon's office to have a drain removed from the surgical site. The drain is a catheter that removes unwanted lymphatic fluids. Hoping to receive the results of the lymph node testing, we were disappointed to find out that they were not ready. Hence, Dan and I would have to sit tight for the time being as the worry and concern lingered.

We returned the following week to have my stitches removed and we hoped that we would receive some positive news. We waited for the surgeon to provide us with an updated assessment and share with us the pathology reports. When awaiting results in the past, I would often experience anxiousness and nervousness, and this day was similar. Sitting anxiously and nervously in the examination room, Dan tried to reassure me that whatever news we received, we would deal with it by forging ahead. In the back of my mind I kept thinking of the 'what ifs.' I worried, "What if the cancer has spread? What if I am too sick to be at our daughter's wedding?" These thoughts kept flashing through my mind.

The surgeon slowly opened the door and walked into the examination room and greeted Dan and me with a smile. He opened my folder containing the information that we were anxiously awaiting. He scanned the report and looked back at us. I held my breath, my heart pounded, and I could feel my nerves fluttering throughout my body. At last and with reassurance, the doctor modestly stated, "You caught the cancer in its early stage. I see no evidence of lymph node involvement!" I let out a breath, knowing that another of my prayers had been answered.

Dan and I were grateful for those encouraging results, but our excitement and joy were short-lived. Despite the positive news, we were not out of the woods just yet. The next day we had an appointment with a medical oncologist from the Windsor Regional

Cancer Clinic who would oversee my case. She assessed the surgical area and reviewed the pathology report with us. I was diagnosed with a hormone-induced type of cancer. Therefore, I was also prescribed Letrozole, a drug which reduces hormone production in your body.

Lastly, we were informed that a sample of the tumour would be tested for the oncogene. This genetic test had proven to be essential in determining the best course of treatment for the patient. If this testing scored on the lower end, no further breast cancer treatment would be required. On the contrary, if it came back in the higher range, I would be at greater risk of the cancer returning. In this case, chemotherapy treatments would then be recommended for me.

The results from this testing took four to six weeks to complete. Clearly, I knew what that meant – more waiting, more wondering and more worrying. It was mid-February 2022, and we would not have the results until mid-March at the earliest. The possibility of having to go through chemotherapy treatments once again after having experienced these taxing therapies 35 years earlier was unsettling.

In the meantime, Dan and I waited patiently and anxiously for the oncogene test results. It was now March 24, and Dan and I were scheduled to meet with my oncologist for a checkup and to obtain the test results. We sat in her office eagerly wanting to learn what we would be facing in the future. When she entered her office, I took a deep breath and looked for signs or any change in her expression. Her expression gave nothing away.

The oncologist then disclosed that the score of my test was 11. We quickly thought, "Was that a good or poor number?" She proceeded to explain that the number was in the low range. Relieved and very satisfied, Dan and I recalled that the lower test score signified that I would not require further treatments. We felt our nervousness dissipate, and we sensed some reprieve knowing that I would only need to take the hormone-suppressing drug. Nonetheless, we were thrilled to learn that no other form of chemotherapy would be called for. Eliminating this factor allowed us to look to the future, envisioning a smoother path. With fewer obstacles, Dan and I could now move forward to help plan a destination wedding for our daughter!

Forging Ahead

Signs of Support

Faced with yet another cancer in December 2021, I had a new battle in front of me. Several of my family and friends referred to it as 'overcoming another hurdle.' That statement resonated with me, as many years ago when I was in high school, I was a member of our school's track and field team. Ironically, the main event that I competed in was none other than hurdles. Dan, Jenna and Justin took the opportunity to make light of an otherwise worrisome situation. They would add cleverly, "You ran hurdles for several years and you were able to clear them then. Now you have another hurdle to overcome. You can do it!"

I embraced those words of encouragement as they gave me strength and motivation to confront the disease. Additionally, I felt that Dan and the kids had my back – they truly were confident that I could clear a new hurdle.

This was a precarious time in our lives. Family and friends may not have realized that expressing their messages of comfort and sharing their words of inspiration were so valued and appreciated by me. For instance, when my niece commented, "Well, this is not your first rodeo," I felt encouraged by it. I sensed that she believed that I had experience in dealing with adversity and that I was prepared to do so once again.

At this time, our lives stood still for a moment, not unlike during my previous cancer diagnoses or the loss of our stillborn son. It was important to understand that there were kindhearted people who took time out of their busy schedules to offer messages of support. It was simply enough to know that we were being thought of, and that was vital to lifting us up and to boosting our spirits. In effect, it kept us going.

During this unsettling time, Dan and I looked for whatever light-hearted moments came our way to relieve some of our anxiety. One such instance occurred when I went for preoperative tests at the Breast Cancer Clinic at Windsor Regional Hospital. I found myself sitting in the waiting area alongside several other women who were also nervously awaiting their tests. When the technologist came to the waiting area to call in the next patient, observing privacy guidelines, she quietly called out the name, Belinda. Upon hearing this name, a lady who was seated across from me stood up. Perplexed by seeing this, I also stood up.

The technologist looked at the lady, then looked at me and sarcastically asked, "You both have the name, Belinda?"

The lady and I looked at each other in a surprising way then we looked back at the technologist as we both nodded. Confused, the technologist then asked for Belinda B.

The lady nodded confidently, stepped forward and said, "Oh, that is me."

I looked discreetly toward the technologist and stated softly, "I am Belinda B, too."

By this time, the three of us were chuckling at the coincidence of both patients having the same uncommon first name along with the same last name initial. On the third try, the technologist whispered the last name, Borrelli. I then came forward and by this time, we all knew that the technologist finally had the correct patient. It was comforting to know that a little humour can go a long way to help lift the spirit in trying times.

In that same period, I observed around me and discovered that there were many women who had been recently diagnosed with breast cancer, several of whom I was quite close to. My aunt, my cousin and several friends had just faced similar diagnoses, and I believed that they were experiencing concern, worry, fear and apprehension – comparable feelings to those that I was going through. However, what was so enlightening and encouraging was how strong and optimistic these women were. Their hopeful attitudes and their positive outlooks provided such inspiration to me. I regarded these women as role models. I believed, "If they could do it, I could do it too!"

In addition to the fortitude displayed by these women, a colleague of Dan's also exhibited great strength after being diagnosed with breast cancer many years ago. This teacher had worked with Dan for several years when Dan learned of his uncommon illness. Given that breast cancer is significantly rarer in males, fewer clinical trials exist making this cancer more challenging to treat. Nevertheless, each time we ran into each other, he and I would share health updates, and I could see the joy in his eyes and hear the positivity in his voice. We felt the connectedness in our special bond. We were both cancer survivors. In brief, whether it was the rarity of breast cancer in males or the prevalence of breast cancer in females, I felt amazed and encouraged by the strength and resilience shown by these people.

It was after my personal breast cancer diagnosis and upon witnessing the bravery of these men and women that my outlook on life gained further perspective. Naturally, as with any cancer diagnosis, I was worried and fearful of the health implications and what the future held. I was anxious about being well enough to be present at Jenna's wedding. I was concerned about overshadowing her wedding plans or the event itself. Without a doubt, I felt embroiled in my inner conflict. Despite all of this, I chose to redirect my focus on positive energy and hope for the future. I endeavoured to screen my worries and concerns from those around me so as not to take others down. During this time, I tried to sulk less and to smile more. In short, I felt that being upbeat, optimistic and hopeful generated more positivity and the belief that I would come out of this alright.

Emotional Impact

Finally, with anticipation and trepidation, the day of surgery arrived, and I remembered the date well. February 3 was both my sister-in-law and nephew's birthdays. In addition, my nephew's wife was scheduled to give birth to their son on this exact day in the same hospital! It was a long wait for Dan and me between the early morning lymph node procedure and my actual mastectomy surgery. In the meantime, our nephew and niece were anxiously awaiting the birth of their son. Several hours later, we received the good news that our great-nephew had safely arrived in this world! His birth made me reflect – every difficult situation has an element of hope. I noted silently, "Yes, every cloud has its silver lining."

With that thought, the nurse called me in for surgery.

Before I knew it, my sedation wore off and I found myself in a conscious state. I glanced around what was now the recovery room and realized that my cardiac issues withstood both the anesthetic and the surgery. I felt surrounded by this sense of immense relief. I also thought back to the silver lining comment and remembered that a new life had entered the world. All of this was a physical and emotional victory for me. I felt so grateful having overcome my first of two hurdles in this race, namely, that I had made it through the surgery. Now, I had to wait for what the results would show.

During this wait time, I was pleasantly surprised that the recovery from the breast cancer surgery exceeded my expectations, aided by the healing practices of yoga and meditation. Thinking back to the day of surgery, I knew it would be less of a challenge to fit in an early yoga session. The real test would be in the days following surgery. The uncertainty of my condition after surgery would play a role in what I could or could not do. The morning after surgery, I felt quite well, and I was determined to attempt at least some form of yoga. I specifically selected one of the *Yoga with Adriene* sessions that focused on lower body and core areas, and I felt proud that I was able to handle it with moderate exertion. To summarize, I found that in my recovery, yoga provided me with the physical and mental benefits, while meditation helped me with relaxation and the emotional impact of the mastectomy.

Two weeks after surgery, I returned to the surgeon's office to have my stitches removed and to receive results. At that moment, I was feeling a little overwhelmed. I was nervous about the removal, worried about the results and anxious about the emotional effect. On an emotional level it is important to realize that each person is unique in dealing with this personal matter and there is no right or wrong. As I lay still on the table, the surgeon gently removed the bandages and then he followed by removing the stitches one by one causing little pain. I waited a few seconds and then hesitantly, I looked down. My first reaction was one of surprise. Not feeling so troubled or upset by what I saw, I was relieved to feel comfortable in my own skin. However, only time would tell the true tale.

After several years had passed, I was very satisfied to confirm that my feelings had not changed from that initial reaction. In an otherwise tough situation both physically and emotionally, I felt I had experienced two wins; a successful recovery and acceptance of my appearance.

On a side note, in regard to breast reconstruction, before making a final decision, I wanted to take some time to determine whether my initial feelings would change. About one year later, I was scheduled for two independent consultations. One was to take place in Toronto and the other was in Windsor. Due to the radiation therapy to the chest that I underwent 35 years ago, the procedure was not going to be straight forward. The procedure in Toronto involved three separate surgeries whereas the one in Windsor involved two surgeries, notably with uncertain results. Without knowing what future health issues I would be forced to face, I felt very relieved that at that time, I decided against having breast reconstruction.

Shifting Focus

In the two-week period prior to our follow-up visit with my surgeon, I faced another challenge beyond the physical aspect, namely, that the breast cancer had not spread to the lymph nodes. As you may recall, our daughter was getting married in the summer in Canmore, Alberta, and I so hoped to be present to witness this special event. Typically, planning for a big celebration like a wedding can be nerve-wracking and anxiety-inducing. The reality is that life is so relative. On the contrary, the nerve-wracking and anxious feelings that we were experiencing had less to do with wedding planning and more to do with waiting for pathology results. To manage the anxiety and worry, Dan and I tried to keep our minds busy. Therefore, instead of getting nervous or anxious about planning for our daughter's shower and wedding, we used it as our outlet.

During that follow-up visit, when Dan and I found out from my surgeon that the cancer had not spread to the lymph nodes, our relief and gratitude were not in short supply. My recovery was continuing to go well and with the added positive news, we took the chance to ask the doctor a question. We asked him if it would be safe for me to travel. He looked at us with an uncertain look on his face. He proceeded to tell us that he would give us the clearance on one condition. We waited for that condition. "As long as you take me with you," my surgeon responded amusingly.

The following day, I had an appointment at the cancer clinic with my oncologist. The visit precipitated another waiting period, this time for the results of the oncogene testing. You may recall that this test was an indicator of cancer recurring. I felt encouraged that my oncologist also cleared me for travel as she stressed that Dan and I would not know about the results for another four to six weeks. There was not much we could do then, but wait to see if chemotherapy treatments would be part of the future plan. Resolved to that fact, we returned to wedding planning as our outlet. It was at that point that we decided to travel with our daughter to Canmore, Alberta in March 2022. We wanted to take care of any onsite plans and to make any necessary arrangements for the upcoming July wedding. We made the choice to move forward for the present time and to enjoy the moment. Then we would deal with what was yet to come.

The trip out west was not only productive, but more importantly, it was therapeutic. For those of you who have travelled to the Rocky Mountains and their surrounding areas, you will know what I mean. I had recently read about 'ecotherapy' and its related effects. Ecotherapy is a therapeutic treatment that uses nature to help one heal. I realized that that was what we experienced on that trip. Breathing in the cool, fresh mountain air, hiking snow-covered trails and admiring ice-clad lakes brought us a sense of joy, calmness and inner peace. Dan and I felt the connection to nature, and we knew that it provided the healing formula for what was needed after what we had been through over the last several months. Time stood still for the moment, and we allowed it to.

Spending time in nature and experiencing its beauty was enhanced with the presence of our daughter by our side. The added support that Jenna provided to us was welcomed and certainly helpful. We spent special times together reflecting in nature and wedding planning. These times generated many positive emotions and created feelings of well-being for the three of us. Although the pending results of the oncogene testing always remained at the back of my mind, the support of my family within a pure and natural setting helped to reduce stress and anxiety that I was feeling during a precarious time.

In April, several weeks after returning from Alberta, I was thrilled to learn that I would not be required to undergo chemotherapy treatments (other than the prescribed Letrozole drug). I could finally accept that I had realized my hoped-for goal. Being 'cured' gave me a renewed belief that once again I was a whole person. With cautious optimism, I felt assured to leave my medical concerns behind for now and refocus on what in life held special meaning for me.

What I valued most was my family. I felt victorious that I was able to remain part of it. I wanted to get on with life and Jenna's upcoming July wedding gave me something to look forward to without having the added weight of awaiting medical test results. I reminded myself of my long-standing belief that when life is good, enjoy it, because it may not last. Life was good at that moment, and I planned to enjoy it with renewed enthusiasm!

July 15, 2022, finally arrived and the time leading up to it was met with eagerness and sheer anticipation for the special event about to happen. Dan and I were happy to take on an active role to help Jenna and her fiancé, Cameron, with the wedding planning. When faced with our health struggles, the planning kept us busy and involved and equally important, we enjoyed doing it.

The morning of the wedding, we awoke to a beautiful, bright day with the sun making its way over the mountains. There were many special moments that we felt blessed to be a part of. As Jenna and 'her girls' were getting ready, we heard their laughter and witnessed their enthusiasm. Similarly, Cameron and 'his boys' were excitedly readying themselves for the big day. I had an excited feeling that it was going to be a great day.

At the outdoor ceremony, we were touched by those close family and friends who were able to make the trek out west and we felt surrounded by their love and support. As the ceremony began, I remember looking up. The sun was shining in the bright sky above the backdrop of the majestic Rockies, soft acoustics could be heard in the background and the pale blue bridesmaid dresses were flowing in the light breeze. The groom's eyes sparkled when he spotted his beautiful bride. Her smile lit up the runway as she walked down the grassy aisle accompanied by her emotional father. The bride and groom were both beaming. I was in awe, and my heart was so full. I have seen it written that you are 'in control of your happiness.' That day proved to be a prime example of Dan and me taking control of it – at least, for that moment in time.

Five months after being diagnosed with breast cancer and wondering whether I would be able to attend my daughter's wedding in Canmore, Alberta, Canada, I made it! The expressions say it all.

One of my proudest moments as a mother was when Jenna married her love, Cameron. Our expanded family that now included Jenna's husband, Cameron and Justin's fiancée, Faith, made my heart full.

Chapter 9

A Skin Oddity

During one of my proudest moments as a mother, I was able to be present to witness the marriage of my daughter to her husband in the striking setting of the Rocky Mountains. Apart from this, in the week leading up to the July 2022 wedding, I unassumingly discovered a sore, ulcerated spot on my vulva. With strong encouragement from Dan and my daughter, Jenna, I hesitantly went to get the spot checked out while we were in Calgary, Ontario. After having the ulcer examined, I was prescribed an antibiotic ointment and was instructed to follow up with my primary care provider back home in Windsor if it did not go away.

Upon returning to Ontario following the wedding out west, I was relieved to find that the ulcer was no longer there. Over the course of the next year, I continued with my regular checkups and diagnostics with the various doctors I was seeing at the time. I met with my local cardiologist, Dr. Mikhail, after my routine six-month echocardiogram. I continued to have my osteoporosis and bone density situation monitored by my endocrinologist. My breast cancer surgeon saw me six months post-surgery for any new signs of cancer. Lastly, Dr. Shoemaker, my London cardiologist, ordered a series of heart-related tests to check on the status of the cardiac disease. As all of these appointments were taking place, I noticed that the small, tender, ulcerated spot on the vulva appeared once again.

After spotting the inconspicuous lesion, I repeated the antibiotic treatment and after several days, the spot disappeared. However, this process would clear and resurface a few more times and with each recurrence, skin pigmentation was also detected in the area. I tried to figure out what it could be, but my numerous guesses were as good as anyone else's. Totally at a loss as to what it could be, I had no other option, but to see my primary care provider. At that

point, after meeting with my doctor, I was then referred to a gynecologist, a specialist in the field, to further investigate the issue.

Luckily, I was pleasantly surprised to learn that I would be
referred to my previous gynecologist, Dr. Hasen. I felt relieved and
comforted knowing that he would bring his empathy to the forefront
in this sensitive situation. It was hard to believe that it was almost
30 years ago that Dan and I met with Dr. Hasen shortly after the
stillbirth of our son, Jordan. Imagine, after all those years, when we
saw Dr. Hasen again, he had not changed. He remained the same
smiling, caring, compassionate person that we fondly remembered.

After being examined, Dr. Hasen offered a few possibilities about
what the ulcerated area could be, the last of which was startlingly
squamous cell carcinoma or the more serious melanoma. To be
honest, of all the possibilities that Dan and I thought, cancer was not
one of them. My mind began racing, and thoughts and questions
emerged. "How could I have cancer in that area? If it were cancer,
what then? What surgery and/or treatment would I need," I wondered
confusingly. The only way to determine definitively was to biopsy
the ulcer. And that is what was done.

The biopsy took place in May, ten months after Jenna's wedding.
Once the tissue was removed, as anticipated, Dr. Hasen was unable
to provide any more information about what the pathology report
might show. I would have to endure the wait for one to possibly two
weeks for the result.

Another Waiting Game

One week passed, and Dan and I were anxiously waiting to hear
back from Dr. Hasen's office. No call came in, so we decided to
contact the office to see if the pathology report was in. Making that
phone call was never easy. It made me nervous. The receptionist
picked up the phone; I gave her my name and told her the reason for
my call. She put me on hold so she could refer to my file. The wait
on my end seemed so much longer than it was. My heart was racing,
and my mouth was dry as I waited for her response. Finally, she returned. Much to our dismay, the report was not yet ready.

The apprehensive feelings that Dan and I experienced while
awaiting these test results brought back memories from the past. We
tried as best as we could to live life normally, whatever that meant,

and not to dwell on the 'what ifs.' Despite our efforts, it was often easier said than done. A few days later I called the doctor's office again, but unfortunately, there were no results. The receptionist suggested to keep trying every few days and could not understand why the pathology report was taking so long. Every few days we continued to call and every few days we received the same response; they did not have any results. This wait not only seemed long, but it was very long. Finally, twenty-three days following the biopsy, I received a personal call from Dr. Hasen. My heart started pounding. Quickly I thought, "Of all the things it could be, I hope that it's any one of them, but one."

Dr. Hasen told me, "It is melanoma." My heart sank. I was not prepared for this assault on my physical and emotional being. I felt a sudden lump in my throat, and my limbs weakened. I had been gut-punched again. I thanked Dr. Hasen and gently hung up the phone.

I took a deep breath before delivering the dismal news to Dan. Without hesitation, I let him know that I received a call from Dr. Hasen. I told Dan that it was indeed melanoma. Dan's expression changed. He turned solemn. I knew that behind his seemingly tough exterior lay the hurting interior. I remember Dan hugging me, his eyes welling up with tears. He simply said, "I am so sorry that you have to go through this." Nervously, I continued to tell Dan what Dr. Hasen reiterated to us in his office. He said that if it were melanoma, I would be referred to London as it was not something that could be handled in Windsor. Dr. Hasen would therefore be referring me to a gynecologic oncologist specialist. Dan's once bold expression was no longer bold.

The wait was finally over, and Dan and I then knew for certain what the mysterious spot was. I do not know what it was about the timing of biopsies, pathology reports and weddings, but we certainly had some experience in this area. Looking back, my first lymphoma diagnosis preceded my sister's wedding by one month in 1987. The next diagnosis of breast cancer occurred several months prior to our daughter's wedding in 2022. This time around, we received the most recent melanoma diagnosis 11 months before our son's wedding day set to take place in May 2024. Had I not known any better, I would have thought that a connection existed between these isolated events.

This current diagnosis brought us back to the drawing board. Not unlike my previous diagnoses, we learned many years ago that when faced with a health challenge, we could not tackle that challenge alone. After considering our options, we began our newest battle by contacting our trusted friend, Dr. DeRose, to update him on my current health status. We also sought out his advice and guidance on how to proceed. His long-standing display of empathy and compassion never ceased to amaze us. This time was no different as he offered us a much-needed sense of relief. Dr. DeRose reassured us that we would be in the best of care in London when he directed us to a well-known and very well-respected gynecologic oncologist, Dr. Sugimoto.

In the meantime, Dan and I conferred with my cousin who worked in the administrative office at the Windsor Regional Cancer Centre. She was very empathetic to our situation and wanted to help wherever possible. She was gracious enough to check with her head of oncology to ensure that a referral to Dr. Sugimoto was made. The assistance, guidance and direction from her and from many other caring people gave us the assurance that we were not fighting this battle alone.

A Third Surgery
Things happened very quickly. Before we knew it, Dan and I were driving up the 401 Highway to make yet another trip to London, this time to have a consultation with Dr. Sugimoto. We were told by many people how compassionate and kindhearted Dr. Sugimoto was. However, we did not know to what extent until we had the pleasure of meeting him for the first time. Dressed in his professional attire with his signature bowtie, he affectionately smiled and tried to comfort us in our moment of desperation. He commented on how he had received calls from the oncologist at the Windsor Regional Cancer Centre, from Dr. Hasen and from his colleague, the well-respected Dr. DeRose. We sensed that he was impressed by the care and concern that we had received surrounding my case.

Prior to meeting Dr. Sugimoto and knowing fully the long list of health challenges that I had faced in the past, I knew that I needed a doctor who would be compassionate and look at my case and be willing to give it his best shot. True to the words of many, Dr. Sugimoto displayed the utmost empathy toward us not only in view of our past health issues, but now with the situation we were currently facing. He understood our justifiable concern and apprehension. Furthermore, he explained, "considering everything that you have been through, you are entitled to have those feelings."

I just remember thinking, 'entitled?' "Wow, that's quite a significant word," I noted. In that instance, I felt that if anyone could help me heal, I believed it would be Dr. Sugimoto. I also had faith that he was not going to give up on me.

I listened carefully as Dr. Sugimoto proceeded to describe his proposed course of action. He would be performing a vulvectomy, a removal of the vulva and surrounding tissue along with the removal of lymph nodes in the left and right groin areas. Overwhelmed and weighed down by all of the information, I tried to refocus.

Dr. Sugimoto continued. He explained that the lymph node removal would be required to determine whether the melanoma had spread to the lymph nodes. I quietly thought, "There is so much to process. But I have to hang in there." When all was said and done, I trusted that if Dr. Sugimoto concentrated on my physical survival, I would focus on the emotional part.

Dan and I then met with Dr. Sugimoto's nurse for additional details. His nurse was a very warm, caring and kindhearted healthcare provider. She thoroughly explained what to expect before, during and after the surgery including how to prepare for the procedure. We were to expect a call from the London hospital shortly giving us a date for surgery within the next few weeks. Suddenly panicked, I realized this was all happening very soon. Fortunately, throughout our visit, the nurse understood our fears and concerns. I am not sure if she realized the supportive role she played in that moment. During this uncertain and trying time in our lives, she gave us hope.

On June 29, 2023, three weeks following the consultation with Dr. Sugimoto, Dan and I found ourselves making the familiar journey back to London, notwithstanding some issues. As luck would have it, our car did not start prior to our departure and in a pinch, Jenna offered her car for us to use. Upon our arrival to the hospital, I was to complete any necessary pre-surgery instructions before the next day's surgery. If all went well with the surgery, it would be an outpatient procedure, and we would be returning home the following day after a brief recovery. At best, that was the plan.

The next morning, I awoke early after a decent sleep. It felt like déjà vu of the breast cancer surgery. Was I nervous? Yes, I was. It was another surgery in which I would be put under and that made me feel anxious and tense too. I had flash backs of 16 months earlier. I had similar feelings then concerning my cardiac condition and how much it could withstand the effects of surgery. Equally worrisome was what the surgeon might encounter during and after the procedure. Here I was again, facing that same inner conflict and I recognized that the uneasiness I was feeling was justified.

Dan and I made it to the hospital in plenty of time and we were directed to the surgical floor. Upon arriving on the floor, I changed into a hospital gown, was laid down on a hospital bed, answered many questions and lastly, was started on an IV. Dan was at my side the entire time and then shortly after, I was surprised to see Jenna walk in. Without her car, she was able to get a ride from her friend who happened to be travelling to London that day. Jenna arrived early that morning to see me off and to be with Dan for moral support. Justin was out of the country completing another travel nursing assignment and felt badly that he was unable to be with us, but I understood.

As I sat in silence for a moment, all the feelings from the mastectomy surgery returned. I tried to suppress my nervousness, apprehension and anxiety using my breathing techniques, but only to resurface a short time later. Before long however, it was time to go into surgery. When Dan and Jenna gave me a kiss and wished me well, I felt sad as I could sense their worry and concern. Uneasily, they each whispered, "I love you," and with that, I was whisked off to the operating room.

In the operating room, I met a female doctor who was going to assist Dr. Sugimoto with the surgery. She was very personable and bubbly and she spoke with an accent familiar to me – Australian I wanted to say. She proceeded to ask me a few questions testing my understanding of what was about to take place. I was also introduced to the anesthesiologist, a friendly gentleman who explained his role. With the infusion of the anesthetic and without knowing, I was quickly sedated. After what seemed to be a short sleep, I awoke in the recovery room.

I took a glimpse around. I felt disoriented and drowsy and slowly,

I realized that I had made it through the surgery. It was chilly, but gradually, my intense feeling of relief warmed me up. As I continued to come out of the sedation, it was comforting to be greeted by Dan and Jenna in the recovery area. I felt quite good, but I was still foggy. I knew enough to realize that my battle was not over just yet. With much anticipation, Dan, Jenna and I waited to meet with Dr. Sugimoto to hear what he had to say.

A short time later, Dr. Sugimoto came to the recovery area and shared the preliminary news. Nervously, I tried to focus and listen intently. He explained to Dan and me that the surgery went well and that he felt confident that he had removed the affected area as well as the surrounding tissue including several lymph nodes on both sides of the groin. Still fatigued, I was able to pick up the essence of his words and with that, I felt intense relief. Nevertheless, he reminded us that the pathology results would tell the full story. Lastly, Dr. Sugimoto indicated that as long as I remained stable in recovery, I would be able to go home that night. Erring on the side of caution, Dan already had a room in London booked for that evening should any unforeseeable circumstance occur.

A Minor Setback

Not long after Dr. Sugimoto left us, Dan was sitting quietly by my side. All of a sudden, Dan noticed some blood on my sheet. He swiftly lifted the sheet and to our shock, there was a pool of blood coming from the incision on the left groin side. Several experienced, astute nurses hurriedly came to apply extreme pressure on the site in hopes of stopping the bleeding, but to no avail. The bleeding continued to gush out. While Dr. Sugimoto was in another surgery at the time, his assistant was paged. Unable to solicit the assistant, my nurses continued to apply intense pressure.

Luckily, a short time after his surgery, Dr. Sugimoto quickly came into the recovery area. He took over applying maximum pressure on the site. After several unsuccessful attempts to stop the bleeding, Dr. Sugimoto pulled Dan to the side. He explained that to properly take care of the bleed and to avoid causing unnecessary pain, he felt it was best to bring me back to the operating room. There, I would be sedated again so that he could stop the hemorrhaging and insert a tube just above the groin incision to allow for excess fluids to properly drain. Dan put his complete trust in the hands of Dr. Sugimoto and gave the doctor his full consent.

When I learned of the new plan, I simply said, "You do what you need to do." All along, my concern with the surgery was the stress that the whole process would place on my heart – to be put under, to undergo the vulvectomy and to come out of the surgery in relatively the same state as I entered it. Little did anyone know that I would have to be sedated once again. I prayed that the procedure would stop the hemorrhaging and that my heart would get me through a second surgery successfully. The nurses would prepare me for the surgery as Dr. Sugimoto prepared himself and his team for round two.

A short time later, I was wheeled back into the operating room. The female doctor with the charming Australian accent cheerfully met me with the same bubbly personality that I had noticed several hours earlier. She said reassuringly, "You are a pro by now and you know the process."

The same anesthesiologist teased that no introductions were required since we all knew each other and he was confident that I understood his explanation the first time around. He exclaimed, "Let's get this done!" I felt slightly nervous and tense again for the next procedure. Fortunately, the effects of the first anesthetic had not fully worn off so my current drowsy, sleepy state helped to ease my nerves. Seeing and hearing all the doctors' lighthearted gestures further reduced my stress level and put my mind at ease, two factors crucial to feeling calmer and more relaxed.

In a timeframe much shorter than the previous procedure, so I was told, I was returned to the recovery room. Again, I came out of the sedation feeling groggy, dazed and weak, but I welcomed being greeted and comforted by Dan. I looked around. I recognized the drapes of the recovery area and realized that I was out of surgery. I felt relieved that my worst worry was over. I had come through another surgery. The nurses explained that during surgery, the team was able to stop the bleeding and that I now had a drainage tube inserted to prevent unnecessary fluids from accumulating in the body. In my groggy state, I tried to make out what Dr. Sugimoto and his team had done.

Dr. Sugimoto came in shortly after to see how I was doing and to explain the latest procedure. His empathy was on full display as he repeated how badly he felt to put me through a subsequent procedure, but he added that he felt better with the results. I knew he cared about me, the person, and I had put my complete faith in him. If he felt the best course of action was to bring me back to surgery, I was in full support. With the additional procedure, he said that I would be admitted into the hospital overnight to monitor my situation.

That evening and the following day proved to be quite interesting. I did not know what to expect post-surgery, but I thought I would be somewhat mobile. However, the surgery made it very difficult to walk due to the significant swelling and bruising. I also had to be very aware and careful of potential infection. I certainly did not want to add any other new ailments to my plate.

Unexpectedly, my biggest challenge and frustration wound up being the drainage tube. I was told that the skin surrounding the tube could not completely form a seal. Hence, the small gap constantly leaked. The nurses tried their best to keep the area as dry as possible to prevent infection, but it was a tall order since the area continued to drip.

The next morning when Dr. Sugimoto arrived for his daily visit, it was not unexpected that he recommended that I stay an extra night in the hospital to keep a close eye on how things progressed. For the remainder of that day, the challenge to keep the drainage site dry persisted thus postponing my efforts to begin walking to improve my overall circulation. It was a catch 22. The more that I walked around to work on my circulation, the more that the area leaked. The more that I kept the area dry, the less circulation I would be experiencing. It was frustrating and I felt I was fighting a losing battle.

As usual, the next day Dr. Sugimoto came in for his routine rounds. After checking on things and evaluating my progress, he sensed and appreciated my frustration over the leaking site. He then sat down to take time to address my concerns. After answering my questions and describing the situation in layman's terms, I felt more comfortable, and I understood that it would take time to heal. On that note, after seriously thinking about it, he recommended that I stay another night in the hospital. Trusting in the doctor's expertise, we accepted his advice. With the drainage site leaking persistently, it was best to be where the situation could be closely monitored and addressed if needed.

Ironically, for what was to have been an outpatient procedure, I was spending my third night in the hospital. Even though I knew it was best for me, I must admit that it was disheartening to know that I would be spending yet another night there. I was not ready for a multiple night hospital stay and was therefore not fully prepared with personal items and clothing. Typically, during my previous hospital stays, it was always uplifting and made me feel better to be dressed out of the traditional hospital gown and to wear my pyjamas or comfortable clothing. However, in this instance, not only did I not have extra attire, I realized that it was much more practical to stay in the hospital gowns provided.

I remained in the hospital for that third night all the while the nurses continually checked on the drainage tube situation and changed dressings often and as needed. Moreover, with the help of Dan and Jenna, I got up to walk occasionally so as not to compromise my circulation. It was comforting and reassuring to have them there during my recovery. Sometimes we take our loved ones for granted, but in every one of my past rough patches, I knew I could always count on them. Dan and Jenna's support was invaluable for not only the physical piece, but more importantly for the emotional one.

The following day, we met with Dr. Sugimoto, and he felt quite confident that Dan and I could handle my situation from this point on. On that note, I was relieved to learn that I would be discharged. The swelling and bruising was very slowly improving day by day. The area around the drainage tube was still weeping, but he suspected that it would last for the foreseeable future. Only after the amount of leaking fluid reduced to small amounts could the drain be removed. I was nowhere near that point as significant amounts of fluid were still draining. The nurses packed up ample supplies to carry us through the next few days. Also, I felt more secure that I would be receiving home care to clean, sanitize and ultimately to remove the drainage tube when it was time to do so.

By this time, Jenna had already left when Dan and I made the well-known trek home. Cushions and pillows made the trip home more comfortable and bearable, but when we arrived home at last, I thought, "There's no better place to be than in my home." As I settled in, Dan looked around and came up with ways to convert our place to one of recovery. While evening descended and I got ready to go to sleep, I calmly reflected, "There's no better feeling than sleeping in my own bed."

Over the course of the next few weeks, it was a challenge to adequately balance the drainage tube issue with maintaining a healthy amount of exercise. I found myself in a similar catch 22 situation that I faced earlier in the hospital. I needed to walk to improve circulation and cardiac wellness. Conversely, movement caused the drain site to leak more. The more that I remained stationary to reduce drainage, the less much-needed exercise I was getting. It was a daily struggle and not before long, I noticed that the area surrounding the tube was slowly getting sorer and more dis-coloured.

Waiting for More Results

Dan and I did not want to press the panic button, but if the site was infected, we wanted to act on it quickly so we contacted Dr. Sugimoto. We made an appointment to see him so he could properly evaluate the situation, and we also hoped to get results from the pathology report. It was two and a half weeks following surgery and the drainage tube was still in place, but most importantly we were anxiously awaiting results. Throughout the recovery, I did not have a good feeling about these results. It appeared to me that the healing process was taking longer than I had hoped and fluids were still draining from the site at a significant rate. I also developed lymphedema or swelling in both thighs due to excessive fluid buildup. As we tried patiently to wait for these results, we knew that an infection would mean a minor setback whereas discovering cancer in the lymph nodes would mean a major one.

Shortly after we were called into the doctor's office, I was examined, and Dr. Sugimoto also checked the condition of the drainage site as well as the amount of fluid that was being removed. There was still fluid draining from the lymphatic system, so he recommended that the drainage tube remain in place for the time being. The surgical site looked good and the site surrounding the drainage tube did not appear to be infected which was very welcome news to Dan and me. Extremely tense at this point, we just needed to hear about the pathology report. Dr. Sugimoto asked us to meet him in his office indicating that it would be a more comfortable setting to talk.

Dan and I presumed what that meant. While I got dressed, Dr. Sugimoto stepped out to see another patient. A short time later, we went to his office and waited for him to return. As we nervously waited for results, Dan and I did not exchange much dialogue. We looked around the room and just sat there quietly. We could hear his voice in the hallway as we continued to wait and we knew that it would not be much longer.

Finally, Dr. Sugimoto entered his office along with my file. Dan and I braced ourselves. We held our breaths as if to prepare ourselves for what we were about to hear. He began by explaining the nature of the lymphatic system and how it worked. Meanwhile my heart was racing, and I could feel my limbs weakening. Taking note of our worried looks, suddenly, he exclaimed, "Oh I do not have your results yet."

Dan and I modestly chuckled, allowing us to breathe more easily. Dr. Sugimoto could sense our huge relief. It was not that we were out of the woods yet. Nonetheless, at least for that moment, there was some reprieve, and we could breathe a sigh of relief knowing that we would not be receiving bad news at that time.

Almost five weeks after my surgery Dan and I had not yet received the pathology report regarding the extent of the melanoma. We thought waiting three and half weeks for the biopsy results was long, but this one surpassed that wait. In that time, the drainage site wound up getting infected. However, antibiotics readily and successfully took care of the infection.

Meanwhile, we tried patiently albeit anxiously to wait for results. Again, we did our best to keep our minds occupied and keep ourselves busy, but there was often that weight hanging over us. Frequently my mind would wander and I would try to prepare myself to receive negative news. Then I would start asking myself questions. Would I need radiation treatments? Would I need chemotherapy? Would it be a combination of both? Would further surgery be required? I would then need to refocus and try to convince myself to hope for the best, but prepare for the worst.

Dan often described the waiting period as mentally exhausting and this one, in particular, was distressing. At last, on August 3, thirty-four days following surgery our wait was finally over. Dan and I received a call from Dr. Sugimoto's office. It was his caring nurse. Again, we braced ourselves. In her compassionate tone, she delivered the news that we were long hoping and praying for. She shared with us that the area surrounding the surgical site was clear and there was no sign of cancer in the lymph nodes! She explained that there would be no further surgery, and no radiation, no chemotherapy and no immunotherapy required! Unless one has been through the waiting process, it is difficult to fully appreciate the joy and utter relief we felt after receiving this good news. For the time being, we could rid ourselves of the mental exhaustion and we could move forward with cautious optimism.

Forging Ahead

Take Control

Over the course of many years throughout my life and especially when new health conditions presented themselves in a number of different ways, awareness was the key. I found that it was important to know and to be familiar with the physical aspects of my body. I felt the need to check and monitor myself for any unusual developments and for any new symptoms or signs that might indicate that something was not right. Did I become more aware of even subtle changes? I certainly did. At times did I become overly sensitive to some changes? Yes, I did that too. I tried to be vigilant because after experiencing many health issues, I did not want to miss the signal of any past illnesses resurfacing or any new ones developing.

Being connected to and aware of my body was very important, but knowing when it was time to act upon a particular condition was also crucial. It was seldom a situation in which Dan and I were certain about how to react to the current issue. Usually we would assess the problem, and we would try not to overreact. Finally, we would determine whether we needed to take action. The same held true for the current lesion issue. After several unsuccessful attempts of treating the chronic spot only to have it reappear, the situation became more concerning. Dan and I now felt that it was time to act and to seek further medical attention.

In early June 2023, once the melanoma diagnosis was confirmed,

Dan and I conveyed the news to family and close friends. From care and empathy to mostly shock and disbelief, we felt the myriad of reactions that we received. Not surprisingly, many of those same people, especially females, were very curious about how I even found the spot in the first place. They asked questions to help them learn more about this melanoma and how it was detected in such a sensitive area. It was important to answer their questions and to acknowledge any concerns they may have had. I was by no means an expert, but I shared whatever information I had. In short, my advice to them was to be aware of their bodies and to be their own best health advocate.

Shortly after learning of my new diagnosis, I remember thinking, "As long as I had a chance, I would do whatever it took within my control, to survive this." Whatever I had the power over when making decisions regarding surgery and treatment options, I would decide. Whatever I needed to do in my post-surgery recovery to keep me as healthy as I could be, I would do. I realized that the part that was within my control was about me and I asked myself, "What could I do to make things better for me?" Facing yet another health hurdle, I was determined to do my part to fight this battle.

As I stated, factors regarding my current health challenge that I had control over helped me to feel empowered in managing my health. Conversely, I also found it extremely beneficial and healing to shift my focus on others. At a time when I was going through my personal trials and tribulations, I knew that many family and friends were facing their struggles. Dwelling on my problems was not going to benefit me and would only serve to take me down. Instead, I tried to use that energy to be sensitive to others and to show empathy and understanding towards their challenges. Not only did this outward focus distract me from what I was dealing with, but it gave me a sense of reason and meaning to my life.

A prime example of shifting focus on others occurred when a friend of mine had been diagnosed with cancer that unfortunately had metastasized. This lady was part of a larger group of high school friends who had reconnected many years after we graduated and a few years prior to her first diagnosis. Although I remained tight knit with a few of these friends long after graduating from high school, there were several others that I had not seen in years. She was one of them. Rediscovering those old friends and rekindling our relationships was special and provided an extra source of support for all of us.

Having only recently received my melanoma diagnosis, I felt the need to be supportive for my friend who was now in palliative care. Along with another reunited friend we made the solemn visit. On that visit, we mainly listened to our friend and few words were exchanged. Our stay was brief. However, I sensed that my purpose was to be there for her and to shift my focus on someone who was in more need than I was. That sense was correct as on the following day, our dear friend peacefully passed away.

The passing of my special friend coupled with my newfound diagnosis made for some concerning and worrisome times. Attending the funeral mass for my friend made me think of and remind me of my mortality. As I listened to the moving eulogy delivered by her daughter, I wondered, "What legacy would I leave behind?" In addition, in these trying times, I thought of my surgery that would determine next steps including what, if any future treatments I would need. In those uneasy times I had remembered a message that resonated with me. "Life is 10% what happens to you and 90% how you react." (Swindoll, 2023) In essence, you may not have control over what happens to you, but you can take charge on how you deal with it.

Be Optimistic

At the time of my diagnosis, I experienced a steady stream of varied thoughts, one of which was optimism. With this news emerging just a year and a half after the breast cancer diagnosis, I recognized that these health struggles would become a common occurrence in my life. After shrugging my shoulders, I chose to take a big step forward and to make the most of a bad situation. It was all about mindset. My thoughts, my behaviour and my outlook would focus on the positive. This would make up the 90% portion of how I would try to manage what happened to me. I must emphasize that this was not always easy to do. Nevertheless, I was determined to do my best to maintain a positive mindset to keep myself upbeat and to uplift those around me.

For instance, that positive attitude was displayed the day Dan and

I broke the news of the melanoma diagnosis to my family. It certainly did not happen the way that we had planned. To begin with, the family was not aware that I had gone for a biopsy. This time around, we felt that it was not necessary to cause them undue worry before knowing for certain what we were dealing with. Secondly, we wanted to let Jenna and Justin know first. Justin had several 24-hour work shifts whereas Jenna was involved with many activities and events taking place toward the end of her school year. This made breaking the news to Jenna and Justin before the rest of the family a challenging feat.

With the summer and vacation time fast approaching, we were left with few options. Dan and I decided to inform Jenna, Justin and my whole family at the same time. As it turned out, we were all getting together for a picnic the first weekend in June. Given that everyone was going to be there including my mother, my sister, my brother-in-law and my brother, we made the decision to let the family know then. The only drawback was that we had planned the family picnic to celebrate my mother's 87th birthday.

So when was the positive attitude displayed? Dan and I were nervous, but tried to keep upbeat as we anxiously waited for the appropriate time to tell the family. As I had stated earlier, there was never a good time, but regardless we summoned the courage. We were forthright and honest as we broke the news to everyone. Looks of disbelief, shock, worry and concern stared back at us. As my family struggled to accept this new reality, Dan and I wanted to avoid signs of pity or sorrow for us. After a few tears were shed and supportive hugs were shared, Dan and I hoped to allay their fears. This was supposed to be a happy event and after taking the family down, we were going to try to bring some humour to the day to lift their spirits. Dan and I started with some funny thoughts and shortly after, the family chimed in with some of their own punch lines. Considering the unusual topic, there were plenty of laughs to go around to lighten the mood!

With a supportive group like this behind me, I wanted to think hopeful thoughts and to display a positive outlook. Once the laughter eased, it was comforting to know of my children's and my family's serious concern for my well-being and for the new hurdle that we had to overcome. In the calm and peaceful park setting, each one took me to the side to ask me privately how I was doing and to find answers to the numerous questions that he or she had. Without knowing full well how I was going to clear this hurdle, there was one thing that I knew for sure. I knew that I wanted to maintain a 'keeping the faith' attitude.

No Regrets

It was early August 2023, about one month following my surgery. Although the recovery was longer and more onerous than I expected, slowly, but surely, the healing took place. I felt confident that I had overcome another hurdle. In addition, other than my standard and routine cardiac tests, my heart condition remained relatively stable. For that moment in time, my fears were dispelled, and my mind was put at ease.

Considering the challenges I faced not so long ago, I now had a renewed awareness of the value of life. As a result, my hope was to return to those activities that in the past brought Dan and me much joy and meaning to our lives. Travel had always been one of those activities, one that was personally rewarding to both of us. Once Dan and I sensed that I was on the right track to recovery and with our doctor's consent we made the decision to take a trip to Argentina and Chile. While we experienced some unique wonders of the world, Dan and I were reminded that life is short, and we needed to make every moment count.

In our travels to South America in 2023, we snuck in a kiss amidst the sunset Chilean vineyards near Santiago, Chile.

Enjoying a lighthearted moment in Val Paraiso, Chile.

Seizing these healthy moments in my life, Dan and I took another opportunity to be recharged. We thought that a land travel venture to Greece would provide just that. As noted earlier, on our summer cruise of 2009, our family visited several Greek ports for our 25th wedding anniversary. Unlike a land trip, our cruise provided us with a glimpse and a taste of each of our three ports. This time around, we wanted to experience the Greek islands with more time and embrace the culture more fully.

Dan and I quickly discovered that Greece set the perfect stage for us to re-energize. The island of Crete presented a true insight into authentic Greek culture, cuisine and landscape. The beautiful island of Santorini typified the Disney World of Greece complete with stunning sunsets and spectacular caldera views. Paros was home to quaint traditional villages and sandy beaches that provided the peace and tranquility that we welcomed. Athens, on the mainland, was our departure spot and very deserving of a stay. Complete with historical sites, rooftop lounges overlooking the imposing Parthenon and characteristic districts, Athens was the ideal final destination. We soaked in all that our trip to Greece offered, the history, the leisurely, decadent meals, the overall beauty and mostly the perfect setting to recharge and to feel immense gratitude – for my comeback.

In the fall of 2023, our travels took us to the Greek Islands. The stunning Santorini sunsets never disappoint!

Overall, faced with this latest setback, I was hopeful and determined to overcome another of life's hurdles. With every adversity, you learn from it, take what you can from it and then you grow from it. What did I learn and take away from this melanoma diagnosis? I learned to more closely monitor changes in my body, and I learned to do whatever was in my control to tackle this. Moreover, by shifting my focus more on others and by being upbeat, a more optimistic outlook toward this challenge would emerge for not only me, but for those around me. Also, when my health allowed me to, I did not want to lose sight of pursuing my goals. One of those goals was to resume our travel explorations. In the end, I felt that I was able to grow from this adversity by doing what we all have within us to do, to maintain a positive state of mind and to continue striving for our goals. It is interesting to note how my personal growth would continue to develop as more obstacles got into life's way.

Chapter 10

Lead Up to Cardiac Surgery

Minor Symptoms

Throughout the latter half of 2022, while I was dealing with the mysterious skin lesion, I was also being closely monitored for my heart condition. Thankfully for my cardiologist Dr. Shoemaker and for his astute care, he decided that it was time to refer me to Dr. Chu, renowned cardiothoracic surgeon of London Health Sciences Centre. Dan and I had heard very impressive accounts from numerous patients and colleagues as to Dr. Chu's expert knowledge and skill. Furthermore, he had previously trained with the esteemed Dr. Kiaii, the cardiothoracic surgeon who first consulted with me regarding my ongoing valve regurgitation issues six years prior. We looked forward to being the recipients of Dr. Chu's expertise. However, before meeting with the surgeon, I was required to undergo several tests for Dr. Chu to more accurately assess the status of the heart.

Looking back to January 2023, five months prior to my vulvectomy surgery, Dan and I had our first consultation with Dr. Chu. Meeting with the well-respected Dr. Chu humbled us and we felt genuinely privileged. By this time the results of my tests were in. In summary, the lungs appeared to be working satisfactorily, and the echocardiogram showed that there was a slight increase in the amount of leaking in the valves. Additionally, the CT scan of the heart indicated that I would be fit to undergo the impending surgery.

During a frank discussion, Dr. Chu evaluated and reminded us of the situation. The reality was that I had radiation-induced heart disease or cardiotoxicity that was caused by the previous radiation therapy that I underwent 35 years ago. The heart disease was progressive and there was no cure. Despite this, the valve regurgitation, although worsening, was not affecting my daily living. He concluded that at the current time, the risk of the surgery outweighed the benefit that I would gain from it. Hence, Dr. Chu's recommendation was to delay surgery until more severe symptoms surfaced such as those identified below by the Cleveland Clinic:

Cardiotoxicity is heart damage that arises from certain cancer treatments or drugs.
What are the symptoms of cardiotoxicity?
Symptoms of heart problems related to cardiotoxicity may include:

- Abdomen enlargement (abdominal distension).
- Chest pain.
- Dizziness.
- Heart palpitations.
- Shortness of breath (dyspnea).
- Swelling and fluid retention (edema) in the legs.
(Cleveland Clinic, n.d.)

A mere five months following the consultation with Dr. Chu, Dan and I found ourselves facing another serious cancer diagnosis. The melanoma result caught us completely off guard, as do so many cancer diagnoses and it quickly became our priority. My cardiac condition remained fairly stable, and I was not experiencing significant symptoms therefore, the issues with the heart became secondary, for the time being. Our redirected focus was to deal with the melanoma discovery.

Fortunately, successful vulvectomy surgery and recovery were behind us. With no future treatments required, our priority reverted to the valve regurgitation issues that were looming. It was late September 2023 and Dan and I had, what we would come to learn, our final appointment with my London cardiologist, Dr. Shoemaker.

During our visit, Dr. Shoemaker reiterated that even though my cardiac condition remained relatively stable, the important caveat was that it was not a question of 'whether' I needed surgery, but it was 'when' I would need it. He ordered an echocardiogram, and he informed us that I would continue to see both Dr. Chu in London and Dr. Mikhail in Windsor. Lastly, he shared with us that he would be retiring. Dan and I were left stunned to hear this news. However, our shock soon faded to happiness for him. With mixed emotions, we said goodbye to a relationship built on confidence and trust. Dr. Shoemaker's years of care, compassion and dedicated service to us would be sorely missed.

One month later, in late October, I was scheduled to see Dr. Mikhail for a routine checkup. On that visit I reported that I continued to experience no significant symptoms. Therefore, I was directed to keep up with my regular exercise and to contact his office regarding any unusual developments. On that note, Dr. Mikhail asked me to book an appointment for one year later.

Severe Symptoms

Coincidentally, in early November, I was scheduled for an echo-cardiogram. This test was one that Dr. Shoemaker had ordered during my last visit with him, prior to his retirement. Only a few days after undergoing this test, and with little warning, I started feeling heart related symptoms. I began experiencing increased weakness, tiredness, low energy and chest pressure more so than I had in the past. These feelings were intensifying daily and Dan and I recognized that the symptoms linked to my cardiac condition were becoming more apparent.

The changes that I was experiencing by then were occurring at an alarming rate. The evening of November 7, I was feeling weaker. I had increased chest pressure and a burning sensation in the throat. My anxiety and worries reached new heights. After contemplating next steps, Dan and I decided that it was time to call an ambulance. The paramedics arrived swiftly. They performed an EKG then administered a shot of nitroglycerine. Although no irregularities were detected in the EKG, taking no chances, the paramedics transported me to the hospital.

Once I arrived at the emergency department of the hospital, there were no rooms available in the ER so I was wheeled to a nearby hallway. In ER, I had a chest X-ray done and my Troponin levels were checked. Troponin enzyme numbers could provide evidence of a heart attack. Lying in the hallway of the ER, I continued to wait apprehensively for test results. With no room availability, Dan was forced to wait outside in the waiting room. In the interim, my anxiety and worry persisted as Dan and I looked for answers.

While waiting in separate areas for many hours, the ER doctor informed me that it appeared that I had not had a heart attack. I was relieved. Thus, I strongly hoped that I would not need to be admitted into the hospital. Apart from that news, the chest X-ray did show images of a suspected pneumonia. For that finding, I was prescribed antibiotics to treat the pneumonia. Luckily, no other acute cardiac ailment was found. Chalking up the entire episode to possible anxiety, after 17 long hours in the ER hallway, with great relief, I was finally discharged.

Within days following the unsettling ER visit, Dan and I were scheduled to meet with Dr. Mikhail. With my symptoms worsening by the day, we could hardly wait to meet with him and we were very anxious to find out what the results of the November echocardiogram showed. Due to the serious nature of the situation, getting a timely appointment was crucial.

Urgent Need of Surgery

When Dan and I were called into Dr. Mikhail's office, he gently closed the door, asked us to have a seat and we could easily detect the serious look on his face. Never had we witnessed this worried expression. Without incident, he gave us the inevitable information. The echocardiogram showed a significant decline in the functionality of the damaged valves. Upon hearing the results and sensing Dr. Mikhail's real concern, I felt my fear, despair and depression creep up.

Right away, Dr. Mikhail prescribed a nitro patch and the drug, Furosemide. Furosemide is a water pill used to decrease the fluid buildup and swelling within my body and around the heart. I would be scheduled for an angiogram immediately in London and I would be referred to Dr. Chu without delay. I was then given strict instructions not to exert any undue stress on the heart and to refrain from doing any physical activity. Essentially, I was in urgent need of surgery. For the first time, I felt that my life was in serious danger.

When I stated earlier that Dr. Mikhail would come to play a key role in caring for me and my compromised health, the time was now. He said that he would try to get a hold of an extremely busy Dr. Chu. Dan and I were surprised that he did exactly that. That very same evening, Dr. Mikhail contacted us to let us know that he had reached out to Dr. Chu to explain both the status and the urgency of my situation. We were impressed by this important gesture as Dr. Mikhail went above and beyond the call of duty. He added that we were to expect a call from Dr. Chu's office within a week to get our previously scheduled January 2024 appointment moved up to 'as soon as possible.' Although Dr. Mikhail did not say much more in that conversation, deep down inside, Dan and I felt that he was instrumental in stressing the urgency of my cardiac problems and the need for immediate action.

Dan and I also wanted to update our longstanding friend, Dr. DeRose, on the seriousness of the cardiac condition as he remained interested in my health status. Dr. DeRose also happened to be a trusted friend and colleague of Dr. Chu so we felt that would be our best hope, if any, to expedite the process. Having Dr. Mikhail and Dr. DeRose as our strongest advocates at a time when the circumstances were dire was a godsend.

Whatever was done or however it took place, Dan and I were just grateful that things were happening quickly. The very next day on November 14, I received a call from University Hospital indicating that I was booked for an angiogram in three days. Shortly thereafter, Dr. Chu's office called to inform me that I was booked for a follow-up appointment ten days following the angiogram. Although we were fortunate to get these appointments so readily, they could not come soon enough. My symptoms were occurring more frequently and were becoming more severe. We knew that my overall health was declining rapidly.

As Dan and I anxiously awaited these appointments, I was keeping a very low profile. I remained as inactive as possible so as not to worsen the current deteriorating condition of the heart further jeopardizing my health. These days and weeks of waiting were extremely stressful. Tensions rose and fell. I would experience any combination of symptoms including chest pressure, head rushes, heart palpitations, numbness in the arms, weakness, lightheadedness, throat burning and indigestion. These shifting signs and warnings would arise, many times unannounced and were now increasing in intensity. Faced with mounting symptoms, I felt overwhelmed and weighed down by the uncertainty. There were numerous times that Dan and I would look at each other and seriously wonder whether it was time to go into the ER or, worse yet, time to call an ambulance.

As the symptoms prevailed, Dr. Mikhail had forewarned us that if I experienced any breathing issues, I would have no choice, but to go to the hospital. Fortunately, breathing difficulties did not occur. The symptoms however, persisted making it difficult to discern whether we needed to seek medical attention. Such a situation occurred one evening. I was experiencing head rushes, tingling in the arms, increased burning in the throat and particularly uncomfortable indigestion. Not knowing if these were related to my cardiac condition or due to anxiety, Dan decided to go to the pharmacy to inquire about some possible over the counter medications that might help to relieve my symptoms.

When Dan went into the pharmacy he asked to speak to the pharmacist. As he explained my symptoms to the pharmacist, she repeated them with a puzzled expression. Perplexed yet concerned, she remarked, "I don't think I have any medication to improve the symptoms that your wife is experiencing." She continued, "I think you need to take her to the hospital." Dan was fully aware of the expected recommendation. The ironic part however, was that similar occurrences were happening to me every few days. That would have meant that we would have been going to the hospital frequently during these uncertain times. As it turned out, when Dan returned home, I was feeling slightly better, and we decided against going to the ER.

Four days following my visit to Dr. Mikhail, on November 17, I would be undergoing my second angiogram. As earlier noted, the angiogram was a standard diagnostic to determine if there were any other underlying issues that would need to be taken care of during surgery. Dr. Chu and his surgical team did not want to encounter any surprises.

As you may have recalled, prior to my previously planned surgery six years ago, an angiogram was performed. At that time the cardiologist detected a blockage in the right coronary artery. This prompted the need for a stent to be inserted in the narrowed passageway to open the blocked artery. It was decided at that time to begin by clearing the blockage in the artery first in hopes that the procedure would improve the valve regurgitation problem. That meant to hold off on the cardiac surgery until a time in which my symptoms increased in severity. Contrary to that time, I was now experiencing serious symptoms. Hence, cardiac surgery was imminent.

It was at this time that Dan and I had the pleasure of meeting the cardiologist performing the angiogram, Dr. Bagur. In the preface, I explained the circumstances surrounding my first encounter with him. I described the profound effect that he had on Dan and me not only as a cardiologist, but more importantly, as a person. Had it not been for Dr. Bagur and his motivating energy, I would not have written this book.

Before the actual procedure, Dr. Bagur put my mind at ease by starting a conversation with me, in Italian. He joked with me and he helped me to relax in an otherwise nervous situation. After he performed the angiogram and once I was wheeled back to the recovery area, he then took the time to explain the results to Dan and me.

That is when Dr. Bagur broke the unfortunate news to Dan and me that he had found another severe blockage in the same artery that had been repaired six years earlier. Thus, he indicated to us that he would be making a recommendation to Dr. Chu. Essentially, he would be recommending that a bypass of the right coronary artery be performed during surgery in addition to taking care of the leaking valves. Due to the serious condition of the blocked artery, Dr. Bagur would stress to Dr. Chu the urgency of performing the procedure as soon as possible.

Finally, it was at this time based on my complex medical history and how I was dealing with it, that Dr. Bagur strongly encouraged me to tell my story. He felt it was important to help and inspire others through their personal journey. Dubious of Dr. Bagur's request, I tucked away any thought of writing a book.

Undoubtedly at that moment in time, my priority was to take care of my compromised heart condition and to prepare for major surgery. Dan and I were eager to meet with Dr. Chu to hear his overall assessment of my situation. We wanted to gather as much information as we could regarding this entire complicated process. Our son, Justin, would accompany us to that appointment. Through both his studies and ER experience, he had gained significant knowledge and interest in cardiac issues. Justin would have a much better understanding of my situation and know what relevant questions to ask.

On November 27, my appointment had finally arrived. Dan, Justin and I travelled the well-known road to University Hospital in London. When we arrived at the hospital, I underwent another echocardiogram to determine if there were any changes from the one done one month earlier. We were then met by a member of Dr. Chu's team who let us know that Dr. Chu was away on conference and regrettably would not be available. We were disappointed to say the least, but we also understood that with Dr. Chu's expertise and specialized skill set, he was in high demand.

Instead, it was Dr. Chu's associate who explained the surgical procedure. As the consult continued, the doctor stated that Dr. Chu's team would be replacing two valves and repairing a third one. Besides that, Dr. Chu would be performing a right coronary artery bypass using an artery from either my leg or my forearm. Hesitantly, while I processed the reams of information, I decided on a tissue valve replacement in lieu of a mechanical valve. Although the tissue valves had a shorter life span, I would avoid additional blood thinners and regular lab work for the rest of my life. The associate also addressed our many questions and had me sign the required forms consenting to the surgery. Finally, we asked the crucial question regarding a surgery date. When the associate responded, we were stunned. He told us it could take one to two years! Our jaws dropped.

As an aside, although in Canada, we have a universal healthcare system in which everyone has access to free healthcare, it does have its drawbacks in terms of offering timely access for care.

Surgery is Imminent

A few days following that London visit, I was scheduled for a follow-up appointment with Dr. Mikhail. He wanted to check on how well I was tolerating the new medications. Most importantly, he wanted to review with Dan and me the results of the angiogram and of my most recent echocardiogram. With concern, he informed us that the angiogram showed, as anticipated, another blockage of the right coronary artery nearby the previously inserted stent of six years ago.

Not surprisingly, my most recent echocardiogram painted a

grimmer picture of the leaking valves. Furthermore, it showed that my blood pressure readings affecting the arteries in the lungs were at dangerously high levels. We would later come to learn that a normal reading was between 11 and 20 and mine was at 90! My condition had worsened from just one month ago fully explaining the rationale for the more severe symptoms that I was experiencing.

When Dan and I explained that we could be waiting one to two years for the surgery, Dr. Mikhail shook his head and emphatically stated that I could not wait that long. Although he fully understood our comfort level and confidence in Dr. Chu, Dr. Mikhail knew that I needed to have this surgery done as soon as feasibly possible. He indicated that if I could not get in soon with Dr. Chu, he knew of some expert surgeons in both the Toronto area and in Hamilton, Ontario. At that point, time was of the essence.

As fortune would have it, Dan and I were relieved to learn that we would be able to continue the trusting relationship that we had developed with Dr. Chu. I strongly believe that the severity of my cardiac condition along with Dr. Mikhail's perseverance and Dr. Bagur and Dr. DeRose' advocacy were the key factors in getting me into the queue with Dr. Chu. Dan and I were fully aware that there would be further diagnostics required and several next steps to follow, however, we felt reassured and confident that we were in the best possible hands.

In preparation for the surgery, the months of November and December were very busy. In addition to the angiogram and echocardiogram, I also underwent another transesophageal echocardiogram, a lung test and blood work. Once again, the diagnostics depicted a poorer picture of the condition of my heart, and as a result, I continued to experience significant symptoms. Furthermore, my blood work showed a lower iron level necessitating a return to London for an iron infusion. When all was said and done, the diagnostics were complete, the iron infusion was done, the preadmission work was ready, and I was prepared to go. Despite all of this, we still had no surgery date.

With the holidays fast approaching, there was plenty of anticipation and speculation as to when I would receive a call from Dr. Chu's office to give us a surgery date. Would it be before Christmas? Would it take place after the holidays? Would I have to wait months for it?

Would I recover in time for our son's wedding? During that time, I was extremely cautious not to overexert myself, to do very little and to stay healthy. The last thing we wanted was for the surgery to be postponed due to a virus or worse yet, a cardiac emergency.

As I waited and wondered, I felt a mix of eagerness and anxiety. On the one hand, I was eager to have the surgery done because my situation had become serious. On the other hand, I felt anxious as I understood the complexity and the challenge of what lay ahead. As I tried to sort through these contradictory feelings, Dan waited and wondered with a feeling of hope. Without a doubt, he knew all too well that I was in urgent need of surgery, but he was hopeful that it would improve my situation. Dan felt strongly that surgery would be the start of my 'road to betterment' and thus appropriately coined the phrase. From that point on, that message of encouragement and hope stuck.

At last, three weeks following my angiogram, on December 8, we received the long awaited call from Dr. Chu's administrative assistant. She said that she had a surgery date for me. I waited anxiously for a few seconds, but it seemed longer than that. She went on to tell me that my surgery had been scheduled for December 22, 2023. I anxiously thought, "Wow, just two weeks away and only three days before Christmas." With mixed emotions, I had no choice, but to accept the date!

Forging Ahead

When I was first diagnosed with melanoma six months prior to my scheduled open-heart surgery, I remembered thinking, "Please don't give up on me." I had lived through so many health issues that I did not want to be considered a write off. Along with that, I would tell myself, "As long as I have a chance, I will do whatever it takes within my control, to survive this." Confronting the highest hurdle that I had ever encountered in the past, never did these thoughts ring more true.

Over the last six years, I knew that one day, it would be time to repair and replace the valves that were slowly and steadily deteriorating. I knew that my heart was not healthy and I was fully aware that there was no remedy that would cure the heart disease that had developed – a stark reminder of the damaging effects of radiation and chemotherapy. My only hope was a chance to improve the existing condition. To do that, I would need open-heart surgery which we knew was risky. Therefore, if my healthcare professionals were willing to stick it out with me, and if I had an opportunity to better my current heart ailment, I was determined to give it my best effort.

Perseverance is a powerful quality that even when the road ahead seems long and challenging, you find it within you to move through it. The months of November and December were without a doubt challenging and presented many uncertainties. Each day as my symptoms escalated, Dan and I simply hoped that we would make it to my next appointment. It was not even that the appointment would alleviate the symptoms, but we were just looking for some reassurance from the experts and some peace of mind that I would be alright.

When symptoms got more serious, Dan and I would often wonder whether my condition constituted an emergency requiring me to go to the hospital. As previously noted, many evenings we would sit quietly, so as not to disturb anything. Dan would look at me and ask me if it was time to go in. With uncertainty, I would respond, "I don't think so." Deep down, I would hope that I was right. There were nights that I would pray that I would wake up the next morning. Despite these critical moments, Dan and I knew that we had to persist and keep on going to get us to the day of surgery.

I wouldn't be where I am today if it were not for my devoted and supportive husband.

Determination and perseverance were what I relied upon to help me to reach that day. In Dan's iPhone, on December 22, 2023, of his calendar app, he had recorded 'Belinda's Road to Betterment.' On several occasions he would refer to that entry to instill in both of us thoughts of hope and encouragement. Despite this, Dan and I knew that multiple hurdles existed. Not only did I have to reach the day of surgery, I also had to make it through surgery and then finally, endure the recovery process. It appeared daunting at times, but as challenging and uneasy as it was, surgery was a must.

Like many other times in life when my health hurdles seemed difficult to clear, it was the support of others that helped to lift me. As Dan and I faced a troubling period, I received numerous calls and messages of love and encouragement from family and friends. They affirmed their interest in knowing about what I was going through in the most crucial time of my life. In permitting Dan and I to share our worries and concern, our loved ones played a critical support role. In my most vulnerable moments, I needed that support. Most importantly, not only did I need it, but I could also feel it.

That show of support, encouragement and love could take on several different forms. In one case, it took on the form of bracelets. Several years before my much-anticipated surgery, my niece, Dana, had nicknamed Jenna, Justin, Dan and I, 'Team Taupe,' because our wardrobes and much of our home decor were taupe in colour. That nickname stuck. Prior to my scheduled surgery, our soon-to-be daughter-in-law, Faith, with the help of her sister and niece, crafted six bracelets, each spelling out 'Team Taupe.' These six bracelets, six to now include Faith and our son-in-law, Cameron, exemplified a clear sign of support and symbolized a genuine sense of unity. We were all together in this. It brought 'Team Taupe' together at a time when it was needed most. Clearly, I knew that I had to do it for me but I realized that I definitely had to do it for 'Team Taupe.'

Chapter 11

My Biggest Battle

Cardiac Surgery

I geared myself up for the biggest battle that I would be facing. With my bags packed, I, along with Dan and Jenna left for London. It was December 21, 2023, and Dan and I were extremely thankful that we had made it to the day prior to my surgery. Dan had booked an Airbnb close to University Hospital and one that had flexible stay arrangements. Dr. Chu said that I would be in the hospital anywhere from seven to ten days depending on my progression. I had always figured that I would have a 'ten day' stay due to the complicated nature of my cardiac condition. I also did not want to get my hopes up too high that I would be released within a week. In addition, Dan booked a place that could accommodate Justin, Faith and Cameron as well as other family members such as my sister and brother who would come to visit.

After unpacking our bags in our new 'home' and once I completed several pre-surgery instructions, Dan, Jenna and I set out to have dinner. Following the directions provided to me by the preadmission clinic, I had a light low fat and low salt meal. Little did we know at that time how long it would be before I was able to consume solid foods again. I guess ignorance is bliss. I embraced the special time that I was together with Dan and Jenna. We kept the mood light and humorous, trying to divert our attention from the impending surgery. Nevertheless, the three of us carried a weight on our shoulders as we looked toward the near future.

Later that evening, I finished the last of the pre-surgery requirements before going to bed. As I had always done in the past, only with more emphasis this time, I selected the three things that I was grateful for that day. I remember the first thing that I was most grateful for was that I had reached the current moment. There were days that Dan and I seriously wondered whether we would make it to the day of surgery. Secondly, I was grateful for the constant support of Dan and my family with whom I could not have done it solo. Thirdly, I was grateful for the team of doctors and healthcare providers that I needed to get me through this. I ended with my prayers and that night I prayed that the surgery would be successful. Surprisingly and with little difficulty, I soon fell fast asleep.

At long last, with great relief yet with expected tension and nervousness, I had made it to my surgery. Early on the morning of December 22, Dan dropped Jenna and me off at the hospital entrance. As I walked in and looked around, I noticed that the hospital was neatly decorated for Christmas. The gift shop was full of whatever decorations and holiday treasures were remaining with only three days left before Christmas.

I observed patients, their caregivers and healthcare workers moving about their daily lives as if oblivious to the holidays that were fast approaching. It was so strange how relative life is. Dan and I had not had much of a chance to think about Christmas and the holidays as our minds were focused on my health. The holidays that year seemed so much less relevant. Our priorities were to deal with both the symptoms that surfaced and with the major surgery that I would soon be facing. The most important thing to us at that time was to be able to undergo the surgery before anything more serious unfolded.

After checking in at the admitting office, I was taken to the pre-surgery area to be prepared for surgery. As usual before any of my previous surgeries, I was asked many questions. In addition, an anesthesiologist explained to Dan and me what would be taking place. I recalled an earlier prior pre-admission meeting with another anesthesiologist from Dr. Chu's team. She complimented me on providing such a detailed medical history. However, I thought to myself that if I did not regularly update my health information over the last many years, I would have never remembered the particulars. We reviewed my history once again as part of the preparatory work.

Dan and I answered a series of questions and listened to as much surgical information as we could retain. I was reminded that I was a patient with a complex medical history going through a complicated surgery affirming my current fear and anxiety. In spite of this, I tried to remain upbeat, positive and cheerful to those caring for me. Knowing that my operation was not going to be a standard case, deep down, I was nervous and scared. Even so, as I lay on that hospital bed, I do not think I fully grasped the gravity of the surgery or the true peril of the entire situation that I was facing.

During the entire pre-surgery preparations, because there was only one visitor allowed in my area, Dan and Jenna would alternate spots to be with me. It was a tense and emotional time for me as well as for them, so it was so comforting to have them close by. Emotions were heightened when Dan received an unexpected call. Sitting close to me, he put the phone to my ear and I was heartened and touched to hear the voice on the other end. It was Justin. He had caught us just in time. Still feeling nervous and scared, I sensed his calming effect.

In a soft-spoken voice, Justin simply said, "You got this mom. I love you."

Not long after the call, it was time. It was considerate of the nurse to allow both Jenna and Dan to say their final good-byes. Jenna hugged and kissed me. I could see the tears in her eyes, and I could sense the unease in her voice when she quietly said, "I love you mummy."

I softly said, "I love you too."

It was now Dan's turn and by this time, the tears were slowly starting to roll down. His look of concern and worry were obvious. In that moment, it was clear that he was coping with thoughts of me not making it. After an emotional embrace and kiss, he could barely get the words out. Finally, he tenderly murmured, "I love you."

As Dan struggled to speak, I knew he was not finished. I nodded, recalling his message of hope. I gently whispered back, "Road to betterment."

With those heartfelt thoughts and loving images etched in my mind, I clung tightly to those last spoken words. Suddenly, it hit me. The threat of not seeing my loved ones ever again unleashed feelings of extreme sorrow and fear. I realized the harsh reality that this could be it. I was then wheeled into a fate unknown.

The ride was short, but once I arrived in the clean and sterile room, I remember feeling cold, tense and powerless. My heart was racing and my body felt weak. I observed many healthcare staff scurrying around busily getting things ready. Each person knew his/her role and each person went about to complete it. Dr. Chu was talking with a number of members from his team and explaining the plan of attack. I continued to feel nervous and apprehensive, but I tried to remain as settled as I could considering the serious surgery that was about to take place. Amidst the nervousness and apprehension, I did feel a true sense of faith and trust in the expert ability of Dr. Chu and his skilled team. I knew that I could not be in better hands.

I did not have much recollection beyond that. Conversely, I did recall one particular doctor who came to my side. He was going to assist Dr. Chu with my surgery and he reassured me that I was going to be alright. As I turned my head slightly, I was deeply touched and truly moved by who I saw. It was Dr. DeRose. In a flash, I thought back to all the medical and emotional support that he had provided to me throughout my life. Unexpectedly, I felt a sense of peace come over me. Soon after receiving his calm reassurance, the anesthetic took immediate effect.

I was so lethargic and slow to come out of the medically induced coma that I had been placed into. Finally, I was becoming more co-operative, and I was able to process some simple instructions, two things that were necessary for my ventilator to be removed. Dan was thrilled to share the news with my sister and brother who were anxiously waiting back home in Windsor for updates. In addition, he was eager to report the following message to them, "Belinda just squeezed our hands, wiggled her toes and nodded when I asked her if she was in pain. If she responds this way with more consistency, the doctors and nurses will likely remove the ventilator tomorrow."

Dan continued, "This is the BEST Christmas present ever, one day late!"

Unconscious State

For the past four and a half days, I was so heavily sedated that I had no memory of what took place nor did I realize how I felt. Unable to remember what transpired, I was forced to rely on my family for the details of both the surgery and my ensuing unconscious state ...

Prior to the start of the surgery, Dan was informed that it could take anywhere from six to eight hours. As anticipated, about nine anxious hours later, Dr. Chu and Dr. DeRose came out of surgery and spoke to Dan and the kids to update them that the surgery was complete. They also reassured the family that they were pleased with the outcome. They further explained the medical process. According to plan, two valves had been replaced, one valve was repaired and that the right coronary artery was bypassed using an artery of my left forearm. In addition, due to the severity of the heart disease, a permanent pacemaker would likely be needed. With those details, Dan and the family were as happy and relieved as they could possibly be, all things considered.

The following day, on December 23, I was in the Cardiac Surgery Recovery Unit (CSRU) in the Intensive Care Unit, a specialized area where cardiac patients are very closely monitored. I was still completely sedated, but in stable condition. Dan was further briefed on the surgery and learned that it ended up being longer than scheduled which was not totally unexpected. It was not out of the ordinary for complications to arise during such a difficult procedure. Apparently, after the briefing with the surgeons, I was brought back to the operating room to stop some uncontrolled bleeding. This necessitated the administration of blood transfusions. Consequently, the whole process lasted a total of 12 hours. Hence after the healthcare team successfully managed these problems, the hope was that I would come around the following day and that the doctors would start weaning me off the latest medications.

It was December 24, Christmas Eve and Dan received several updates. My heart function, without machine assistance, was looking quite good and I was breathing mainly on my own with some assistance from the ventilator. These were two very good signs in the recovery process. Therefore, the plan for that day was twofold. Firstly, the plan was to remove the high-tech device that helped my heart pump blood. Secondly, it was to reduce the sedation medication so that I could be taken off the ventilator. Furthermore, Dan was once again informed that a permanent pacemaker would likely be needed to regulate my heartbeat. Not surprisingly, because of that news, I would be spending some additional days in the CSRU.

During my family's vigil, to say that those days in CSRU were difficult would be an understatement. Throughout this induced coma, the doctors, nurses and support staff worked tirelessly to *provide the best possible care for their critical patients such as me. I was attached to medical equipment that allowed me to breathe and that helped my heart beat more consistently. I was connected to many lines and tubes to help drain fluids and to provide life-saving medications and nutrients. It was a delicate balancing act between many factors including heart and pain medications, heart rhythms, blood pressures and lung pressures. There were so many variables involved that had to be constantly controlled with the utmost precision. This continual testing of the healthcare team added to the overall challenge.*

In those trying periods, Dan, in particular, was having a tough time managing and taking control of his emotions and feelings. He found himself coiled in his thoughts and as the taxing days passed the coil only twisted tighter and deeper.

During that strenuous time in intensive care, Dan was fortunate to not only have the much-needed support of Jenna and Justin, but also of their spouses, Cameron and Faith. As overwhelming as it was, Dan and the family continued to keep a watchful eye on monitors that displayed vital signs, pressure readings and heart rhythms. They actively asked questions intent on knowing all they could about what was going on. As the entire healthcare team closely monitored my condition, making even minor adjustments as required, it was no doubt that the recovery was demanding for all involved.

Further to the support they already offered, Jenna, Cameron, Justin and Faith convinced Dan to go out for Christmas Eve dinner together. Hesitantly, Dan agreed on the condition that he would return to the CSRU after dinner. When Justin suggested that he did not need to return, Dan replied, "You don't understand, Justin. There is no place I'd rather be."

With that, Justin knowingly said, "I can't argue with that, dad."

As the five family members gathered for dinner, Dan felt comforted by the kids' presence. At one point, they individually shared a personal anecdote that each of them had experienced with me in the past. Some of the stories were touching, most of them were funny. It was an important bonding time for all of them, but particularly for Dan. It was heartening to spend quality time together with the kids. On that note, Dan's emotions soon turned to tears when he was re-

minded that someone was missing.

On Christmas Day, Dan and the kids were looking forward to receiving the one gift they had been wishing for and had been so anxiously awaiting. They longed for me to finally come around from the induced coma. It had been three long and very intense days for my family. For me, I was so sedated that I had no idea what was happening, nor did I have any knowledge of the seriousness of the situation. However, for my family and for my loved ones back at home, I could not even begin to imagine what they were going through. It was demanding and especially tough on Dan, Jenna and Justin waiting for me to wake up day in and day out with no success.

The Christmas holiday was a quieter day for all concerned including healthcare staff, patients, caregivers and visitors, so there was less action taking place in the hospital. Nevertheless, some of the tubes and machines that I was connected to were removed. In addition, the nurses persevered in preparing me for coming out of the induced coma. This action would then be immediately followed by the removal of the breathing tube.

For this process to occur, I was slowly weaned off of the sedation medications and was then asked to follow several simple instructions. Evidently, I was unable to complete even the most basic tasks such as nodding my head, squeezing someone's fingers or moving my toes. I was still quite agitated, incoherent and uncharacteristically uncooperative. After several unsuccessful attempts throughout the day, the nurses unhappily concluded that it was not the appropriate time for me to be brought to a conscious state. My family stayed as long as visiting hours allowed which was just before the nurses' shift change. Hence, my family left disappointed that they had not witnessed me emerging from the induced coma. Their Christmas wish was not granted.

Disheartened, when Dan, Jenna and Justin left the hospital they decided to get something to eat for their Christmas dinner. They soon found out that no restaurants were open due to the holiday. Luckily a small grocery store provided the necessary source of nutrition that they needed. After returning to their accommodation to have dinner, Dan felt more comfortable returning to the hospital to check up on me and see how things were going.

Upon Dan's arrival, Dr. Kumait, a member of Dr. Chu's team,

knowing how upsetting it would be, gently broke some news to Dan. Due to the length of time that I had not yet come out of the induced coma, the doctor recommended to Dan that I have a brain scan done to rule out any brain bleed or dysfunction. It was a gut-wrenching blow to Dan. He was speechless. Shocked and distraught to hear this, he was overcome with emotion. The doctor tried to reassure Dan that he did not think that I had suffered any brain damage, but he had to be certain.

Devastated, Dan thought to himself, "This cannot be how the story ends." He shook his head and kept reinforcing that belief in his mind.

Shortly after coming to terms with what was to take place, Dan contacted Jenna and Justin to inform them about this unsettling update. Learning of the latest news released feelings of shock, confusion and fear. Suddenly a sense of doom hovered over them. Clearly, emotions got the best of Jenna and Justin as well.

Dan waited nervously for the brain scan to be done. He was also informed that preliminary results would likely not be available for several hours. He wandered about the halls of the hospital anxiously awaiting a call from Dr. Kumait. Back at their London 'home,' not being able to think of much else, Jenna and Justin comforted each other and hoped and prayed for good news.

A lengthy hour later, Dan received a call from Dr. Kumait. The doctor temporarily put Dan's mind at ease when he reported that the preliminary results revealed no brain impairment. Not the Christmas gift that my family had initially hoped for, but grateful and relieved for this new gift bestowed upon all of them!

Without exception, the day after Christmas, my family came to be with me in the CSRU. Now less anxious considering the results of the brain scan, Dan and the kids continued to hope that I would regain consciousness soon. It was day four and the nurses pressed on with their efforts to help me come around from the coma. It was to no avail. I was not yet coherent, and I was not able to follow instructions properly. Meanwhile, Justin consulted with his nursing friends who had cardiac surgery experience. Concerned with my prolonged induced coma, he relied on their professional opinion. At this uncertain point, my family became very worried that I was not waking up.

In the meantime, back in Windsor, my mother, sister and brother and other family members were anxiously awaiting to hear some positive news. Far from good news, my current state was not favourable. I was still hooked up to several machines, I was connected to numerous lines and not to mention, I remained unconscious. In addition, fluid retention had reached concerning levels causing excessive swelling in my body. This made me barely recognizable. Worried about the mental impact it would have, especially on my mom, Dan thought it was best for my family in Windsor to wait until I came out of an unconscious state before coming to London to see me.

Later that day, the nurses persevered to get me to comply with basic tasks while Dan, Jenna and Justin became the hopeful audience. After further reducing the sedation medication, simple instructions were again given to me. Dan and Justin tried to have me hold their fingers as they repeatedly asked me to squeeze them. At first, I only squeezed their fingers lightly. They asked me to do it harder. I did! I think I literally hurt them. Jenna was at my feet and she asked me to move my toes. I slowly wiggled them! Dan then asked me if I was in pain. I nodded my head! After being given some additional pain medication, I settled down and I returned to a calmer, more peaceful state. My family was ecstatic that at long last, I was becoming more coherent and more cooperative. I was finally able to complete simple instructions!

Having success in getting me through step one of regaining consciousness, it was now time to tackle step two, removing the ventilator. For this to take place, the sedation medication would have to be further reduced to improve my ability to follow instructions. Only when I was coherent enough to follow the respiratory technologist's tasks would it be safe to remove the breathing tube. Yet I had to be compliant enough to allow the nurses to remove the tube without resistance. What the healthcare team wanted to avoid was to have to re-insert the ventilator when I was in a semi-comatose state.

Several hours passed, and Dan, Jenna and Justin were looking forward to seeing me become more coherent and cooperative so that the ventilator could finally be removed. Not giving up, my family continued to ask me to perform some basic tasks to prove my *compliance. Despite all their efforts, the nurses felt that I was still not ready for the removal of the breathing tube. They indicated to Dan and the kids that they would try again the following day. As usual, my family stepped out at dinnertime for a few hours for the nurses to take care of their routine patient care duties. Discouraged, but more compliant than I was, my family left for a dinner break.*

Upon their return, Jenna and Justin arrived at the ICU zone while Dan remained behind and had a seat in the waiting room. My nurse then kindly said to the kids that for this time, she would make an exception and allow a third visitor. Thus, she called for Dan. As the three of them approached my area, they discovered that the drapes were closed. Showing some concern, my family wondered what had happened during their break. They waited patiently for the nurse to draw the drapes. As she gently slid open the drapes, Dan and the kids saw me lying there. They suddenly noticed that my ventilator was gone! Also, I was in a semiconscious state! My nurse and respiratory technologist proudly showed off their feat. Unbeknownst to my family, they were able to finally remove the ventilator. The nurse and technologist surprised Dan, Jenna and Justin and granted them their best Christmas wish ever, one day late!

Gradually, as I very slowly regained some degree of consciousness, I could indistinctly make out the three figures that were hovering over me, but I knew very well who they were. With the ventilator recently removed and suffering from severe dry mouth and no voice, it was difficult to get the words out. Nevertheless, I was able to get my message across. The last words that I heard from my family before surgery were literally my first words repeated back to them. Barely audible, I tearfully uttered, "I love you," to my three pillars. I then vaguely recalled my worst fear prior to surgery. Now that I was seeing my loved ones again in front of me, I put that fear to rest. Out of sheer relief and elation, my family delicately held my hands, embraced me and they too broke down in tears.

Semiconscious State

Still in a haze and very disoriented in my current state, imagine my total shock when Dan, Jenna and Justin tried to explain to me that it was December 26! I methodically shook my head. In complete disbelief, I tried to process that this was the first time that

I had woken up in four and a half days! Bewildered and confused, I was unable to accept that fact and it seemed incomprehensible to me that I was unconscious for so long. Completely unaware of what had transpired, I tried to absorb the idea that Christmas Eve and Christmas Day had come and gone. Despite that, it seemed so unreal to me.

Aside from my doubts, I continued to fade in and out of consciousness. Somehow, I could still sense a feeling of immense relief that I had made it through surgery. Conversely, not fully awake for much of the time, I would experience vague recollections of things that happened. For instance, I imagined that I kept correcting those around me about the number of cancers I endured. Family and staff would state the number two or three. I would rightfully respond that it was four. Also, in my confused and cloudy state, I would be constantly praising one nurse for being able to move and lift my extremely swollen body. These thoughts, along with many others, randomly floated in and out of my distorted mind.

Somewhere, in between those altered states, I was still able to discern my long-held belief that I would do whatever I had to do to survive this. What was not clearly evident to those around me quickly became more obvious as my loved ones witnessed me repeating the phrase, "I need to do this for my survival." One constant was my commitment to recover. That commitment remained steadfast.

Following the four and a half days of both heavy sedation and unconsciousness, the next hurdle to clear was to become stable enough to be released from the CSRU. Clearing this hurdle would mean that I was ready to be moved to the Cardiac Care Medical Surgery floor. However, the reality was that coming around from the induced coma was not an easy process. It was very gradual and Dan and the kids would often find me drifting in and out. At times, I would become agitated and very delusional. Even though I was now out of the coma, I still could not recall with any degree of clarity what happened in those following days in the CSRU. Therefore, once again I counted on my family to fill me in on what took place ...

On December 27, the day after awakening, as promised, my sister and brother made the trip to London to finally see me. I remained hooked up to many machines and I was still connected to numerous lines. In addition, I continued to experience severe fluid buildup. Hence, it was decided that my mom would visit later when my condition improved. I was still semiconscious, and I had no idea that I would be getting visitors beyond my family. Apart from that, Dan and the kids knew that I would welcome seeing Cindy and Michael.

I did not remember much of the visit with Cindy and Michael, but one such thing stood out. When I woke up every so often, I would robotically express my gratitude in seeing them and I would thank them frequently for coming to visit. I wished that they would not stay long because I wanted them to return home to their families. Just envision that prior to my surgery, my sister and brother had planned to visit me on Christmas day. Due to unforeseen circumstances though, that did not happen. In my mind it was Christmas so each time that I woke up, I sluggishly repeated to them, "Merry Christmas!"

Ironically, for a visit that was so anticipated and that was supposed to be heartwarming and touching, it did not turn out that way. Firstly, Cindy and Michael did not expect to see me in the condition they did. I was still so swollen that they could hardly make out that it was me behind the remaining pieces of equipment, lines and tubes. Secondly, they did not recognize my altered personality. I became annoyed quickly and I displayed such rude behaviour that I am sure made them wonder why they ever came to see me.

In one instance, while Dan was updating my sister on my status, I slowly turned to Michael and asked him to stop talking. Innocent of the offense and dumbfounded, he looked around wondering who I was referring to. Unable to understand what I was asking him; I raised my hand to my mouth and made a talking gesture with my fingers. I then pointed to him. Voila! He understood and stayed 'quiet' for much of the remaining visit!

In another case, this time with Cindy and Dan, they were the recipients of my rudeness. I was requesting something, and they could not make out what it was. They kept asking if I needed lip balm and I continually shook my head. Did they not understand that it was not the lip balm that I needed? Annoyed with the constant repetition of questions, my brother too began shaking his head. Disgusted that my husband and sister could not understand what I needed, I turned to Cindy and whispered, "You are frustrating me."

Being on the other side of my impoliteness and my disrespect could not have been easy, but it did provide many moments of comic relief!

It was not the visit that Cindy and Michael were expecting. On one hand, they were very concerned about seeing me in that current state. On the other hand, they were relieved to see me in a conscious state after having endured what I did. They understood the agitation, impatience and delusion that often accompanies cardiac surgery patients in their recovery. Despite my sister and brother not anticipating seeing such uncommon behaviour from their sister, they were just grateful to see me.

The days following my siblings' visit proved to be important steps in the recovery process. The quality care that I was receiving included careful monitoring of blood pressures, oxygen levels and the ever-crucial blood pressures in the lungs. Any notable oddities or changes that were detected would be evaluated and adjustments would be made as required. In addition, it was time for the speech language pathologist to assess my swallowing and to treat any problems if needed. Along with swallowing, the speech language pathologist would also help my family to better communicate with me. I was having a difficult time speaking. I do not think this support could come soon enough for my family! Nevertheless, I did not pass the swallow test and hence I was not ready to drink fluids just yet. In short, my recovery was progressing, but as expected, at a very slow rate.

It was my seventh evening in the CSRU, and it was time for the nurses' change of shift. Routinely during the change, Dan and the kids would leave to take their break and to pick up something to eat. After dinner, Jenna and Justin decided to stay behind in their accommodation whereas Dan returned to the hospital. As he entered the intensive care area, he was quickly approached by the doctor on call that made Dan aware of a critical incident that occurred while Dan was out. The doctor explained to Dan that my heart had stopped for about 40 seconds. He used the medical term to describe this as asystole.

Once the specialist briefed Dan on the situation, Dan instantly called Jenna and Justin to break the news. When he anxiously explained the incident to them, he repeated the medical term, asystole. Completely confused, Justin responded, "Dad, do you know what you're saying? Because there's no way that mom went into asystole based on how we left her." He was baffled, but continued, *"Asystole means that her heart stopped."*

Dan replied, *"Justin, that's exactly what the doctor explained to me."*

Wanting to get the facts straight, Justin asked, *"Can you let me speak to the doctor?"*

Dan looked up and saw that the doctor was nearby. He politely asked the doctor if he could explain to his son what happened. Dan also made the doctor aware that Justin was a nurse and would be better able to comprehend the incident. In short, the doctor confirmed with Justin that I went into asystole. Dan's interpretation of what had taken place was accurate.

The doctor returned the phone so that Dan could finish his conversation. Justin could not believe what had happened nor could he imagine how critical the incident was. After speaking with the doctor, however, Justin felt reassured that the situation was under control. Justin conveyed to Dan and Jenna that the event had been taken care of successfully leaving all of them with relief and a sense of comfort.

Once the situation had settled down and my condition was now stable, Dan wanted to seek clarity on what happened. My nurse outlined the event in detail. Apparently, the nurse was abruptly alerted by the alarms going off on one of my machines. Suddenly, a complete team of healthcare personnel rushed to my bedside. There was an indication of a heart rhythm emergency that ended up lasting about 40 seconds. She said, in no uncertain terms, that I had flatlined.

The nurse continued to explain that due to the open-heart surgery, rather than performing the conventional, more aggressive CPR, the team needed to use other interventions to resuscitate the heart. These interventions involved using medications and/or probes to stimulate the heart. Nevertheless, she said that before resorting to those options, they carefully adjusted my external pacemaker that I had been attached to after surgery. After closely monitoring the effects of the pacemaker adjustment, the team observed that my heart rhythm had been restored.

In search for the cause of the heart stoppage, my nurse informed Dan that an ultrasound of the heart was also done. It showed that *both the right and left sides of the heart were tired, laboured and were experiencing some difficulties. Despite the weakened heart muscle, adjusting the pacemaker proved to be the solution to restarting my heart. My nurse concluded that the occurrence of the heart stoppage presented a very critical situation. Then she added that this event confirmed that an internal pacemaker would likely be required to prevent another similar situation from happening again.*

The morning after, with Dan and Justin present, an electrophysiologist evaluated the previous day's precarious event. This specialist, an expert in treating irregular heart rhythms, would make the determination as to whether I needed a pacemaker. Due to the uncertain circumstances surrounding the heart stoppage, she made the decision to reassess the situation in a few days to see if my heart rhythm improved. Before introducing another foreign object into my body, the hope was that once the heart healed, the problem would take care of itself. Both Dan and Justin knew that the predicament was not taken lightly.

The visit with the electrophysiologist was interrupted by a healthcare team member who stopped in to see me. He was wearing his hospital attire along with his mask, so he was not immediately identifiable. As he approached my bedside and leaned over to speak to me, Dan and Justin wondered who the person was. When he lowered his mask to ask if I recognized him, it became clear to Dan and me who this individual was.

In my rare conscious state, I very slowly nodded and whispered to him, "You saved me. I love you."

In that emotional moment, he smirked and humbly replied, "Well, I did not save you, but I helped out. I love you, too." He then continued, "Do you remember what I asked of you?"

Again, I slowly nodded and carefully whispered back two words, "The book."

Touched by my response, the healthcare member was moved to tears. Drifting out of consciousness, I was oblivious to the fact that Dan and Justin's tears began to flow as well. After an emotional embrace between Dan, Justin and the gentleman, Justin soon came to learn that he had inadvertently met someone who he had heard a great deal about. It was the ever considerate and empathetic, Dr. Bagur.

Following the heartwarming encounter with Dr. Bagur, we

continued to face numerous days of expected highs and lows. One of those low points was the challenge of regaining strength after the surgery. This was another key step in my recovery, namely, to get back the muscle strength that I had lost during the entire surgical process and intensive care stay. Still extremely swollen, it was crucial for me to get out of bed and move as much as possible to prevent circulation and breathing problems. This was easier said than done. With the assistance of the physiotherapist, nurses and lifting devices, the first step was to get me out of bed and to sit in a chair. After a great deal of time and effort, I finally made it to sit in a chair for a few hours. The feeling of such weakness was disheartening. At times the recovery felt as if I was taking one step forward and two steps back.

Over the course of the next four days in the CSRU, I continued to make slight physical improvements. More lines were being removed and the healthcare team was ridding me of more machines. The physiotherapists and nurses continued to get me out of bed and moving as much as possible. I was slowly becoming more alert, and my speech was gradually getting clearer. In addition, an echocardiogram showed that the right side of the heart was still weak, but that the left side was getting stronger. The valves that had been replaced were no longer leaking. Overall, my heart condition was satisfactory. Although the improvements were minor and slow, it was encouraging for me and my family to see that I was moving in the right direction.

Even though I was getting better physically, my delirium and confusion began increasing as was often predicted. The plethora of medications that I was taking combined with the sounds, beeps and alarms that were commonly heard in the CSRU, could frequently lead to delirium. I was saying things that did not make sense to the healthcare team and to my family. For example, I was certain that I had been recently diagnosed with dementia. Dan and my nurses did not concur with the diagnosis and they giggled, chalking it up to my confusion. In turn, I would simply shake my head. Annoyingly, I would tell myself, "They just don't understand."

Also, being a typical rule follower, I usually towed the line. Though now, I developed some defiance, and I would occasionally refuse treatment. This refusal primarily involved several nurses who *in my altered mind were not properly certified. Dan and especially my children often found me in a foggy state and heard me saying things that they thought were absurd and very funny. Despite the amusing comments, after experiencing several days of my delirium and confusion, my family was anxious to have their old mom back!*

With each passing day, my delirium lessened, and my alertness and lucidness improved. What started as gibberish in the search line of my iPad became more recognizable and I could slowly use the iPad to navigate through Google and YouTube. Not surprising to my family, my initial searches included obituaries, dementia and the late-night talk shows. I was better able to sit up and watch television and to comprehend what I was watching. It felt like such a relief for both my family and for me. We could better understand each other with less confusion and more clarity. Fortunately, their old mom was coming back!

Conscious State

It was New Year's Eve and for the first time since surgery, I began remembering a good portion of what happened during the day. It was encouraging to regain some memory and feel some degree of consciousness and coherence return. I heard Dan explaining to my nurse that he and I had spent the last 39 New Year's Eves together. He asked if it would be possible to remain after visiting hours to ring in our 40th New Year together. The nurse discreetly and kindly obliged. Jokingly, we talked about the three of us celebrating the New Year together in the CSRU with snacks and champagne. I very much welcomed being back, as my mother would often say, 'in the land of the living.'

During the day, I again met with the speech language pathologist to determine whether I was ready to drink fluids and eat soft foods. For the last nine days, I was restricted from having any fluids, including water! I had not passed the swallow test and a week earlier I had developed fluid buildup around the lungs. The risk of excess fluids entering the trachea was too high, potentially causing pneumonia. Therefore, I was not able to have anything by mouth. The situation gradually improved and I was currently ready for the swallow test to be repeated.

The test began with me taking a sip of water. After slowly taking a small sip, I began coughing, almost choking on water. I cautiously gulped down the sip. The test progressed through juice, apple sauce and then pudding. All the while, it was very difficult for me to swallow. Funny how we take such automatic things for granted such as the ability to swallow. It was not until this reflex was taken away from me that I realized how important it was. Astonishingly, I passed the test and I was finally permitted to start drinking small amounts of fluids.

New Year's Eve was quite quiet in the hospital with the New Year's holiday fast approaching. In the meantime, I was taken off of more medications and more lines were removed. I was able to sit up in bed, and with help, I was now able to get into a chair. I was also spending more time sitting up and slowly searching on the computer, topics that were of interest to me. Dan and I recalled statements made by the doctors and nurses. The recovery was going to take time and that meant that it would require a great deal of patience. The very small improvements that I experienced one day after the next were our constant reminders of how true that was.

My nurse must have been busy with other responsibilities, so Dan and I found ourselves alone as the evening was winding down. We were thankful that she allowed Dan to remain until midnight. As Dan and I counted down to the New Year, we reflected and thought back to where we were just a few months ago. Those anxious moments at that time certainly made us feel grateful now. Proudly, we rang in our 40th New Year together!

New Year's Day 2024 was a special one for me as Jenna, Justin and Cindy were coming up to London to be with Dan and me. I was already excited that I was going to see them, but unbeknown to me, I was going to have a spa day as well! When they arrived, their mission was to provide quality care treatment to make me feel better both physically and emotionally. Jenna began by washing and towel drying my hair. Cindy styled my hair as best as she could and put some makeup on me. Justin and Dan provided the comic relief. Not only did my family provide good company, but their visit certainly improved my appearance and lifted my spirits. Taking into account everything that I had been through in the last week and a half, I began the New Year on a positive note. I was comforted by my family's visit and by the relaxing treatment that they provided to

help calm my mind and continue my recovery.

The following day, little by little, I worked on my recovery with the hope that I would soon be moved out of the CSRU. With assistance, I sat in a chair for progressively longer periods, and I tried to drink small sips of water to help with my swallowing. Prior to that time, when I could not have anything by mouth, I resorted to using sponge swabs to rinse my mouth to both moisturize it and to brush my teeth. Again, how common it was to take such standard things for granted such as brushing one's teeth. I also searched the internet which improved both my dexterity and my reading comprehension. My body including my fingers was still very swollen, making it very challenging to simply type out my intended words. Slowly I felt myself improving to a point that I could move forward to the next step – moving out of an intensive care unit onto the cardiac care floor.

Later that morning on January 2, having to return to Windsor for work commitments, Justin and Cindy said their goodbyes. Deep down inside, I was sad to see Justin and Cindy leave. I do not know if they realized how good the previous day's spa treatment felt. I felt refreshed and re-energized, but in particular, I felt better about myself. The battle had been difficult to that point, but their reward brought me peace of mind.

At last, that very afternoon, after spending 11 taxing days and nights in the CSRU, I graduated from intensive care. I received heartfelt goodbyes from the staff who by now had become friends to my family. I was transferred encouragingly to the Cardiac Care Medical Surgery floor with a renewed promise of recovery.

Forging Ahead

With less than three weeks to go before Christmas, Dan and I did not want to get our hopes up for a surgery date before the holidays. It seemed ironic that we were hoping for this major surgery as soon as possible. We, along with our families, anxiously awaited word from London. Finally, we received the much-anticipated call. I would be scheduled for surgery on December 22, 2023, just three days before Christmas. Suddenly, surgery was a reality, and the mental preparation became a priority.

Every situation could be looked at from a different set of lenses. At a time of year when people were doing last-minute shopping, baking Christmas goodies and planning menus for upcoming dinners and holiday gatherings, I was stopped dead in my tracks. Most people were busy and excited preparing for the holidays, whereas I was trying to stay healthy and preparing myself mentally for what I would soon be facing. For Dan and me, that time was bittersweet.

It was a nerve-wracking period as I was facing worsening symptoms, yet we were just pleased that I would be having the surgery done prior to Christmas. Although holiday plans had previously been set in motion with both sides of our families, these plans would soon change, and we would not be part of them. We felt badly about missing out on these celebrations, but we had a different priority that year. Even though Christmas and New Year's would look different and would take on a new meaning, we could not have been more relieved. The way Dan and I viewed our situation was that we had to keep things in proper perspective. In comparison to the alternative, we had no choice, but to get the surgery done before something more serious occurred.

As you may recall, Dan always regarded himself as an emotional person, but prided himself in being strong. Prior to my surgery, he felt confident that he would be alright taking care of me on his own. Due to Jenna and Justin's work commitments, he did not want to take them away from those responsibilities. Essentially, he did not feel that it was necessary to have them accompany him during this difficult experience. Little did Dan know how much he did need Jenna and Justin and how much he would come to value their presence and their support.

A less stressful family moment on the shores of Lake Erie enjoying the simpler pleasures in life.

When your loved one is ill and needing to go through serious surgery, it is often easy for caregivers to forget about taking care of themselves. Caregivers play such an integral role in taking care of their family member, so it is vital for them to stay healthy. Healthy, in this moment, referred to a healthy body, mind and soul. Dan handled the body portion well. During those days in the CSRU, he tried to get adequate rest, maintain decent eating habits and take breaks from the hospital to walk in the fresh air when he needed to clear his head. However, Jenna and Justin's involvement as well as the support of their spouses, Cameron and Faith, were crucial in helping Dan with the mind and soul parts.

In these critical care situations, it was common to see small signs of progression and then to witness setbacks. That is when Jenna and Justin's presence proved to be invaluable to get Dan through the highs and lows of this grueling experience. Not only did the kids provide the emotional support, they also added the much-needed moral support. For example, they offered Dan reassurance and encouragement during the setbacks such as when I experienced a heart stoppage or when I underwent a brain scan. They also provided another set of ears to take in and comprehend the vast information that was being disseminated daily. The range of emotions varied significantly during these trying times and it was comforting for Dan to know that Jenna and Justin were not far away.

See the LHSC brochure, *A Guide for Families* (2010) which highlights caregiver tips for coping and supporting their loved one.

In summary, have your supports in place. You may think that you can tackle these stressful situations alone, but you do not realize the emotional toll that it can have on you. Dan soon realized the benefits of having Jenna and Justin and their spouses around. They lifted Dan when he was down and they helped to heal him when he was broken. Being able to communicate with Jenna and Justin and share personal feelings that only they would understand, provided an effective way of dealing with each of their worries. Not only was it important for Dan to have the support of the kids, but it was equally necessary for the kids to have the support of Dan and of each other. Sharing meals together in supportive company offered much needed comfort for all of them. Essentially the care and encouragement of close family filled a void.

Not only did the cardiac surgery journey have a huge impact on my immediate family, but it had a big effect on our extended family and friends as well. It was a long and rough road for my family observing my health condition change from day to day and at times not in a positive way. As well, it was extremely difficult for our family and friends back home. They waited in the wings for any piece of hopeful news reassuring them of my progress. As our loved ones were concerned and frightened, the emotional impact was significant on them too, especially given that they were not in our immediate presence. It was important to recognize their concerns and worries and to keep them informed and updated as much as possible to lessen their legitimate fears.

One key takeaway from our experience was how touching it was and how much it meant when family and friends took the time to ask Dan how he was doing. Even though I was the patient that was physically going through surgery and recovery, it was a very stressful time for Dan. He was the one who stood by my side, observed numbers intently, listened to monitors, asked questions and waited patiently for any changes in my progress. It was very difficult to watch someone you love fighting through their illness. Months after my surgery, I remembered Dan telling me that one of the most difficult parts was the uncertainty of my mortality. He thought back to a day that I was lying unconscious in the CSRU, and he looked at me with worry in his eyes. He was reminded of how strong my desire was to survive. What concerned Dan most was – would that desire be strong enough?

It is essential to know that the supportive partners need care too. As I stated earlier, they may be putting up a good front when they may be quietly suffering inside.

As noted above, caregiving extended beyond Dan's care and support. Jenna and Justin also played an important role in my recovery. In the weeks prior to surgery, when I faced many serious symptoms, I was hanging on to whatever means possible to help me through that tenuous time. Jenna and Justin knew that my one constant was the comforting, uplifting and encouraging ways of my trusted yoga instructor, Adriene. They were aware that without fail, every single day for the past five years, I met with Adriene virtually as she guided me through a unique experience. Now I wondered how I was going to continue this journey through my cardiac surgery and recovery. I knew that I could participate on the actual day of surgery. I would just have to wake up earlier. Apart from that, after that last morning yoga, the future of my consecutive yoga sessions remained unknown.

That is when Jenna and Justin stepped in. They knew how important it was to me to follow through with my yoga commitment. Thus following my surgery, when I was powerless, they took over. During my most critical moments, hooked up to numerous monitors and lines and unable to move, they connected my iPad to a video and started a session. Day in and day out, Jenna and Justin's resolve helped to usher me through a yoga journey. They began by gently moving my fingers and toes, and then progressed to my hands and feet and then ultimately to my arms. As I slowly came out of the induced coma, the encounters became more independent.

While I gained more strength to use an iPad, I was able to gradually follow the yoga sessions on my own. Frequently drifting in and out of consciousness, I must admit that I did have to rewind multiple times. This prompted chuckles from my family. In spite of the many rewinds, Dan and the kids celebrated any small victory. For me, it was rewarding to fulfill my personal yoga goal, due solely to my family's determined perseverance. It is interesting to note that this perseverance would continue and become a critical piece in helping my family through the next phase of my recovery.

Chapter 12

Days of Delirium

Complex heart surgery, countless medications, irritating equipment noises and peculiar sounds from nearby patients provided the perfect formula for the onset of delirium. Delirium is a confused, disoriented state that typically begins quite suddenly. In my case, that is how the delirium began, almost immediately after I came out of the induced coma. As a result of the trauma to my heart, the numerous medications and all of the strange sounds that I was hearing, the medical team was not completely surprised that I experienced this significant change in my mental abilities.

While I was in this distorted state of being, in my mind I believed that my thoughts, my feelings and my emotions were very real. Unlike to the outside world, those thoughts, feelings and emotions were anything but real. In my altered state of reality, what was obvious to me was confusing to those around me. This caused me a great deal of frustration due to my loved ones' lack of understanding. They could not comprehend what I was saying, who I was talking about and where I was coming from. Clearly, they did not have a clue. It was them who lacked clarity, because it was not me. At least that is what I believed.

The most unfortunate part was that those imagined stories would be shared with those who stood by my side every day, especially during my most critical state. My husband, children, their spouses and later my sister and brother would bear the brunt of my absurd demands, and of my unkind comments. At a time when I should have been most gracious and thankful for their support and for what they were doing for me, I certainly did not show it.

At first, I was not going to write this chapter because there were simply too many of my imagined stories. Secondly, my stories were just that, untrue. However, both Jenna and Justin felt strongly that those stories should be shared. After some careful thought, I decided to write about the delirium that I experienced to make my readers aware of the potential side effects of major surgery. When you combine surgery and prolonged unconsciousness with medications and with unfamiliar sounds, delirium can often occur. In addition, my delirium experience was an eye opening, startling part of my recovery and I realized that I needed to share it. Next, it helped to place my unusual behaviours and my unexpected comments in their proper context. In other words, it helped those around me to make sense of the actions that I was exhibiting and of the narrative that I was expressing. Lastly, the bizarre stories provided some lightheartedness to an otherwise stressful time. For all those reasons, it was time to choose which of the many stories would make it into this memoir.

Imposter Nurse

As I stated earlier, my delirium caused me a serious inability to think clearly. All of these experiences were real in my mind and happened, or so I imagined …

There was a young, dishevelled woman who came to the hospital for an interview for a nursing position in the Cardiac Surgery Recovery Unit. She was being interviewed just outside of my room, so I heard what she was saying to the interviewer. She boasted about completing her undergraduate studies in neuroscience, but also had an engineering degree along with several other accreditations in the health sciences. She concluded by stating that she had a wealth of practical experience working with patients. Needless to say, she got the job.

Shortly after her interview, I overheard her saying to her similarly untidy friend that she got the job. With skepticism I wondered how this young person could have realistically acquired all of these credentials in her short life. In a sinister and sarcastic way she continued and said to her friend that she would be working immediately with patients, me being one of them. Suddenly I became very nervous. I had worked so hard to follow doctors' and nurses' orders to improve my chance for a successful recovery. Now I was going to be cared for by someone who was not even a qualified nurse.

Each time the new 'nurse' came to complete her tasks with me, I refused her care. When my family members were in her presence and she wanted to perform work on me, I tried to let them know through my facial expressions that I did not need her help. I thought that the only way that I could relay to them that she was a fraud was through my piercing stares. Could my family not detect my complete disgust and disapproval? Could they not understand what this person was all about? Unfortunately, they could not see through her.

When one of my nurses would come in to perform her tasks, Dan, Jenna and Justin strived to have me accept her help, but I refused. In my mind she was the scamming nurse who had no expertise or business treating patients. Unable to convince me, they solicited the help of another healthcare worker to do the necessary work. In another situation with that same nurse, she was required to insert an intravenous line. Jenna tried desperately to explain to me the absolute necessity of this procedure, but again, I gave Jenna a cold stare – if looks could kill. After refusing once again, Jenna literally needed to hold my arm in place so that the nurse could finally complete the required task. For someone who habitually complied and who followed rules, my reluctance to do so stunned my family.

Signature Socks

Several of my nurses were extremely kind and caring toward me and I became especially close with them. Three were standouts. I was grateful for their compassion and for their competence as nurses. Additionally, I was touched by the kind gesture they showed me when I was being prepared to be moved out of the CSRU. Each of the three nurses personally signed my bright yellow hospital gripper socks with loving messages wishing me continued health and a successful recovery.

I cherished those socks and the messages that they held. However, when they went missing, I became so disheartened. I surmised that they were mistakenly placed in the dirty linen stand, never to be seen again. Despite my assumption, I asked Dan to search for them because they held such meaning for me. The first obvious place he looked was in my hospital bed. He pulled off the blanket and sheets and was surprised to find that I had one sock on and one sock off.

By this time, I was wearing another pair of non-slip socks, only now one of those was lost. Dan looked high and low around my bed and around the room for either the signed pair of socks or for the newly lost sock, but with no luck. Baffled and clearly frustrated over the missing socks, I asked Dan to give up the search.

Trying to piece together which signed socks that I had lost, Dan tried his best to locate something that he knew nothing about. In his attempt to appease me, he spent a significant amount of time looking all over for those missing socks. Without risking embarrassment, he stopped short of asking the nurses if they knew anything about socks that had been signed by other nurses. Dan resolved himself to the fact that those socks would never be found and that they most likely never existed.

Sweet Clementine

Another of my exceptional nurses took excellent care of me. She was so kind and had the most pleasant demeanour toward patients and staff while at the same time working in a very stressful environment. She always created an atmosphere of trust and made me feel comfortable in her care. I would often witness these qualities firsthand from my bed as I observed her actions when working with others. Similarly, I would notice the respect that was shown back to her. She was a special nurse who knew her calling.

One evening this nurse introduced me to her husband who was just hired at the hospital's CSRU. He was an extremely intelligent person who was contemplating changing careers from engineer to cardiac care nurse. He would be my nurse for the night shift. He was accustomed to working nonstop and working long hours. His request to me was to ask for whatever I needed and to keep him busy. I was amazed at how quickly he learned to complete even more difficult tasks. He would only have to be shown once, and he would know what needed to be done. I heeded his request, and he was kept busy and worked energetically for his entire shift taking care of me and his other patients.

To express my gratitude toward my nurse and her husband, I wanted to buy a gift for their young toddler, Clementine. I solicited the help of Jenna, and I asked her if she could pick up an outfit for the baby in exclusively neutral colours. I also asked her to look for a baby book, preferably one that specifically included the baby's name. Each time Jenna returned to visit me, I asked if she had purchased the baby gifts. Jenna would look at me with a puzzling expression and would try to distract me from the subject matter. She would make me aware that she had not yet purchased the items. She would then double check with me and confirm what I had requested. Dissatisfied, I told Jenna that if she was not able to complete the task, then I would have to do it myself!

When I told Dan and my family of my experiences with the kind-hearted nurse and her newly employed, bright and competent husband, they could not keep a straight face. Dan and Jenna set the record straight regarding the names of these two people and their relationship to one another. Apparently, the two individuals had different names than what I called them, and they were not married to each other. The baby gift request would leave Jenna perplexed and doubtful. She would wonder how to respond to me and would quickly try to change the subject. Jenna knew that each time that she came back to the hospital without the gifts, it would be upsetting to me. Essentially, she did not want me to get worked up given my recent heart issues. Also, during that period, each time that I brought up the baby's name, Clementine, Dan and Jenna could not stop themselves from laughing. Pardon the pun, but laughter was the best medicine.

A year later, when my family and I returned to the CSRU to visit and bring treats to the staff, the charge nurse confirmed what my family had been saying all along. She confirmed that the female nurse and her so-called 'husband' did work back-to-back shifts, but were not married to each other. Apart from that, we learned that the so-called 'husband' did indeed have a child named Clementine. I reassuringly thought to myself, "Perhaps I didn't lose it completely!"

Cream Collection

On one of my sister's visits, she brought me a lovely collection of creams in a variety of pastel colours and scents. I had her place them neatly in a row on the shelf in my room. Each cream had a different name with a different coloured label. The creams were accompanied by a select variety of health and beauty aids. I thought that those were perfect patient gifts considering the dry conditions within the hospital. In addition, the gift certainly cheered me up and helped me to look and feel better.

Each time that I looked over to that shelf, I would admire the attractively packaged creams. When I was moved to a different area of the CSRU, all of my belongings were packed up and brought to my new place. In my new home, I noticed that some of my personal items, including the gifts from my sister, did not follow me. I was certain that those items were left behind in the previous room. I asked my nurse, and she assured me that they would be found, placed in a bin and returned to my new room.

I waited for the return of the items, but they were nowhere to be seen. Later, when Dan came to visit, I asked him to check for the creams. I explained to him in detail the appearance of the containers and I specifically asked for the cream with the taupe-coloured label. He searched around with a perplexed look on his face and then slowly pulled out a tube of toothpaste from my nightstand drawer. I shook my head, I slapped my thigh and thought, "Did the toothpaste resemble the taupe coloured cream?" Very confused, he then pulled out my toothbrush. Again I shook my head in disbelief. Now we were moving further away. Completely mystified, Dan gave up, and so did I.

A few days later, Cindy came to visit. Determined to find the creams, I asked her if she could look for them. There was a nurse's cart in my room that contained three bins. I was certain that my creams and health and beauty aids were erroneously placed in the top bin. I asked my sister to pull out the top bin to retrieve my items. A short distance away, my nurse was sitting at her station making notes on my progress. Cindy looked over to the nurse and then quietly and delicately pulled out the bin slightly. In it she found bandages, gauze, tape and other supplies, but there were no creams. She quickly closed the bin. I shook my head and realized that my things were probably in the second drawer. Without drawing the nurse's attention, Cindy carefully checked the second bin and this time she found masks and gloves. Cindy knew what was coming next so she automatically checked the third bin only to find sterilizing and sanitizing solutions. My room had been scoured quite well and there remained no sign of the creams.

I tried earnestly to solve the mystery of the missing creams. I asked Cindy exactly what she brought on one of her initial visits. She proceeded to tell me that she brought medicated lip balm and several other items. In addition, with a chuckle, she strongly stated that she never brought the exclusive creams and toiletries that I imagined she had. The mystery had been solved. The scented creams and the special items rested solely in my altered state of reality.

Breaking Rules

In my time in the CSRU, I often felt nervous and apprehensive. Ironically, those feelings were not due to the actual illness or recovery. They were due to my family's difficulty in abiding by the visiting hours of the hospital. The hospital had posted visiting hours and when Dan, Jenna and Justin were pushing those limits, I was not happy. As visiting hours drew to a close, I became agitated and anxious if my family members did not leave.

On a few occasions, when Justin came after visiting hours, he would persuade the security guard to allow him to come up to my room. I would be curious as to how he had gained access and he would respond with, "Can I not come in to see my mom in these serious circumstances?" Although I found it difficult to argue with that, staying after visiting hours was not acceptable and it made me feel very anxious and upset.

Jenna was very worried yet very interested in knowing what was happening as I was progressing through my recovery. At times, she would call the hospital after visiting hours to get any updates. In another instance, Jenna and Justin came to visit. Trying to gain a clearer grasp, Jenna would ask the doctors and nurses many questions to get a better handle of the situation. Not wanting to burden the healthcare staff, I suggested to Jenna and Justin to funnel all of their questions through dad. When the endless questions continued, it became more nerve-wracking and I asked Jenna if she could leave. Justin was more understanding and sympathetic than I was and he asked her to stay. However, Jenna did not want to upset me any further, so she decided to follow through with my request and she left.

Dan wanted to spend as much time as possible with me. Very concerned about my status, he would be there throughout the day making many inquiries, monitoring my progress and providing moral support. Nonetheless, when visiting hours were ending, I did not want Dan to stay. He pleaded his case to me as to why I should let him stay, but I did not want him to push it. On occasion, he convinced me to allow him to stay for one more minute and I obliged. He remained for the time being sitting quietly in his chair until the allotted time expired. When the minute was up, Dan reluctantly said, "Goodnight. I love you and I'll see you tomorrow."

My perception of the entire visiting hour storyline was completely distorted. One evening when Dan was visiting, in my disoriented state, I thought that visiting hours were over. I did not believe him when he told me otherwise. So, he solicited the aid of my nurse who tried to explain to me that he still had plenty of time. I was still not convinced and when I asked Dan to end the visit, the nurse was left dismayed. Unfortunately, my concern and lack of clarity with respect to visiting hours made for some disheartening and disappointing times.

Dan, Jenna and Justin were very conscientious about the visiting hours. If on occasion they found themselves visiting beyond the posted hours, they only stayed later with permission to do so. There was no need to sweet talk the security guards. There were no after hour calls unless they went through Dan. Although my family was very concerned about my status and hence wanted to be well informed, on the contrary, they tried to do so without imposing upon or overburdening the healthcare staff.

As I wrote earlier, there were numerous stories that I lived through in my mind. There were stories that I remembered in detail and that were very real to me. There were accounts that were non-sensical and that had me see and believe things that were not present. There were stories that had potentially serious consequences such as the time that I was refusing medical treatment. At last, the illogical stories came to an end and I was able to think more clearly. Fortunately, for my family and me, the delirium that I experienced was short-lived. There was a point in time after the joking ended and the laughter subsided that my family was relieved to have me return to my normal self.

When I began to come out of my delirious state, I relived my stories with Dan. One by one, I described each story, and I asked Dan if it did occur. I asked if there was an unqualified nurse who looked after me. I asked if there were a pair of lost socks that were signed by the nurses. I asked if there was a wife and husband team who worked in the CSRU and who had a baby named Clementine. I asked if my sister brought a gift of exclusive creams. To all of those questions, Dan answered with certainty, "No."

Finally, I asked Dan if he and the family had abused hospital rules and privileges. He responded with a resounding, "No." Learning that all of those stories never happened brought an extreme sense of relief to me. Looking back, even though the delirium caused periods of significant stress and anxiety, I was confident that Jenna and Justin's mom was back!

Forging Ahead

Delirium is quite a powerful state. I learned that delirium can greatly alter your thoughts, behaviours and emotions as I personally experienced. Having knowledge that this could happen given a serious or prolonged illness, surgery and/or medications was not only important, but was helpful too. It was helpful to my loved ones who witnessed me going through it. It was also helpful to me to comprehend the disorder so that I could eventually distinguish between reality and distorted reality. Being fixated on an idea such as breaking hospital rules and displaying distrust such as fearing care from the unqualified nurse were all signs of delirium. Knowing that those were symptoms helped my family and me to better understand what was happening and why it was happening.

At times, the symptoms of delirium can resemble those of dementia, so it is important to recognize the differences. I could have imagined Dan and the kids probably questioning themselves about this topic. After all, in my delirious state, I did tell my family that I had been diagnosed with dementia. For starters delirium comes on quite suddenly. Dementia, on the other hand, usually presents itself more gradually and is progressive, meaning it gets worse with time. Delirium also is typically associated with a medical problem. The symptoms of delirium can come and go and tend to worsen in unfamiliar surroundings which, in this example, are similar to those of dementia. In summary, due to the contributing factors and symptoms that I displayed, my condition was more easily identified as delirium. However, in cases where it is not as readily apparent, it would be helpful to rely on family to provide insight to accurately diagnose the disorder.

Given that delirium severely affected my ability to understand clearly, to remember and to control what I said or did, I literally became a different person. The behaviours and demeanour that I exhibited were quite out of character for me. Therefore, it was necessary for Dan and my family to be especially patient, understanding and empathetic during that trying period. For instance, Dan would explain my uncharacteristic, erratic behaviours to my nurses to justify my disturbed state. Unquestionably it must have been a very difficult time for my family to have to tolerate and navigate my extreme actions and reactions.

Fortunately, as I noted in the previous chapter, my family's unwavering perseverance helped all of us get through my confused state. That perseverance combined with a lighthearted dose of 'just go with it' created a bearable situation for them and allowed for me to safely recover from the delirium. Recovering from this altered state brought me another step closer to ultimately being discharged from the CSRU and being transferred to the Cardiac Care Medical Surgery Unit. I was now ready to put the surgery and ICU experience behind me and look forward toward my betterment – but perhaps, not so fast.

Chapter 13

Road to Betterment

When I first arrived in my private room on the Cardiac Care Medical Surgery floor, I was pleasantly surprised to see how spacious, light and airy the room was. It was a stark change from the draped and windowless rooms of the ICU area that I had previously resided. This room had a large window where the sunshine lit up the space. It was January 2, 2024, and to date we had a mild winter, so the ground was still clear of snow. The remnants of autumn could still be seen with brown leaves and dry, moss coloured grass covering the ground six floors below us. Having a private room with plenty of bright and cheery space did a great deal to lift my spirits. It was also ideal for times that family came to visit. Little did I know at the time why I was specifically assigned a private room. The reason was that sometime during my stay in the CSRU, I came into contact with someone who tested positive for COVID. Essentially, I had to be isolated from the rest of the population.

On the wall of my room facing me hung a white board. It had the name of my nurse and beneath her name was the word, *Goals*. That word stood out and I knew that I would be facing that board often for the number of days that I would be on the Cardiac Care Unit. I began thinking as to what my goals would be. It did not take me long to decide on my answer. My first goal was to build strength, the second goal was to walk three times daily and the third was to eat solid food. The goals would give me something to reach for and that is exactly what I did. Each day I would work diligently toward achieving those goals. This effort would allow me to get ready to be discharged as soon as my health was stable and as quickly as I could function independently.

Over the course of the next several days, although not easy, I made slight improvements in attaining my goals of walking and building strength. I met with the physiotherapist who taught me how to get out of bed. In the CSRU, I had lost significant muscle mass so I had to learn techniques to help me to get up and to stand on my own. To do this, I was given a small pillow to use to relieve pressure on the healing chest incision. Holding the pillow on my chest with my arms crossed, I would use the strength of my legs to power me up to a standing position. At first, I needed a great deal of assistance, but with each new day my legs got a little stronger. Once I mastered the simple act of getting myself up and standing, I could progress to walking. Soon I was able to slowly walk around the hospital corridors with the use of a walker. The physiotherapist also provided me with an exercise plan to work on my own to help prevent soreness and stiffness and to ultimately regain further strength.

On some days, the road to betterment seemed very long and rough. I would look at my inflated arms and at my overly swollen legs and I wondered how or if they would ever return to their normal size. I wondered how I would achieve my goal of eating solid food when I was still on a feeding tube making the swallowing of fluids very challenging. I wondered if I would ever regain the muscle mass in my legs to allow me to get up and walk on my own. I wondered if the pain and soreness in my chest would eventually subside. I felt that there were so many unknowns and so few certainties. Only time, patience and perseverance would tell the story.

Cardiac Crises Continue

One evening while I was sound asleep, I was suddenly awakened by anxious discourse and the feeling of subtle shocks to my upper abdomen. I immediately opened my eyes and looked around. A wide range of emotions hit me. First there was shock and confusion. Then there was disbelief that quickly turned to fear. I was utterly stunned to discover six people, three on each side of me, maneuvering lines, taking and monitoring my vitals and observing my responses intently.

I soon came to learn that I was being reconnected to an external pacemaker through wires in my abdomen. Days before, the external pacemaker had been disconnected to determine if my internal heart rhythm could function on its own. Without hesitation, I asked one of my nurses to contact Dan. Undoubtedly, I knew that he would want to be made aware of the situation. The staff continued to work on me diligently in what appeared to be an urgent and dangerous situation. As the jolts to my abdomen subsided and the concerned dialogue turned to relief, I knew that I had just made it through some crisis.

Not long after, during the night, Dan arrived at my bedside and the cardiologist on call and my nurse gave us the breakdown of what had transpired. Apparently and unexpectedly a critical event occurred. I had flatlined again and suffered a complete heart stoppage of 10 seconds followed by a second and then a third heart pause of eight seconds each. A code blue had been called, but CPR was not administered. The cardiologist noted that my external pacemaker was started up again, hence the feeling of the small shocks that I sensed in the abdomen. He reassured Dan that my health status was now stable and that the team would continue to monitor the situation closely. Evidently, I had indeed been in a crisis. With a look of concern, my nurse admitted to Dan and me that on that night I had given both her and the staff a real scare.

The electrophysiology team was consulted once again. It was critical to note that this flatline episode was more concerning than the one that I had previously experienced in the CSRU about a week prior. Following that second assessment with the electrophysiologist, I was consented for a pacemaker insertion. Although the medical team wanted to avoid introducing something new into my body un-necessarily, the risks of not having a permanent pacemaker were just too great. Considering the potential ramifications of the last two serious events, having a pacemaker would reassure us and provide us with the peace of mind that we needed.

In the days that followed that troubling event, my health progressed slowly, but steadily. My nurse practitioner would meet regularly with Dan and me to give us any health updates and to manage my cardiac condition. From the beginning of my stay on the cardiac care floor, she showed the utmost care and compassion toward us. She was patient with our endless questions and understanding of our concerns. On one such visit, she relayed to us that the medical team was pleased with my recovery to date. This was very comforting to Dan and me. Additionally, she reviewed the goals that the doctors had set out for me: to reduce the fluids around my arms and legs, to have a pacemaker inserted and to improve the condition of the heart muscle. She was pleasant in her approach and thorough in her delivery and Dan and I admired that.

In the meantime, I continued to work on my personal goals of building strength, walking several times daily and improving my swallowing reflex. I continued to meet with the physiotherapist to build my strength and endurance. In addition, much to my relief the feeding tube had been removed. Despite this, swallowing remained difficult and therefore, the visits with the speech pathologist were helpful to improve that reflex. All things considered, it was a slow, but progressive recovery.

Picking up the Pace

Finally, after several days and a few postponements, on January 10, it was time to undergo the insertion of a pacemaker. I was wheeled down to the surgical floor and two very kindhearted and considerate nurses met me and began preparing me for the procedure. They both spoke gently and lightheartedly to Dan and me while they efficiently went about their work. Oftentimes healthcare workers do not realize the positive impact they have on patients in reassuring them and helping them to remain calm and relaxed at an otherwise apprehensive time. In this stressful moment, I embraced all the empathy the nurses provided.

I then met with the electrophysiologist who was assisting in the procedure. She was a young, affable specialist whom I had the pleasure of meeting several days after my surgery during my first consultation with the electrophysiology department. I thought back to that time. I knew that I was often drifting in and out of consciousness, and I had not always been so nice to those who were caring for me. Reluctantly, I knew that I had to ask her if she was one of the individuals to whom I was rude. She kindly responded, "Do you know what you said to me when I met you for the first time?"

I held my breath for a second anxiously awaiting her answer all the while hoping that my words were appropriate. Without hesitation she proceeded to tell me. She said that I told her, "You are my guardian angel. Thank you for taking care of me."

What a sense of relief I felt knowing that the electrophysiologist who was taking such gentle and proficient care of me was treated with the respect that she deserved. After all, in that consultation some time ago, she was just trying to figure out the best course of action for me.

Following an explanation of what was going to take place, the specialist alerted the nurses that it was time to take me to surgery. In the familiar cold, sterile room, the surgical nurses introduced themselves and provided some further explanation about the procedure. They then began covering me with sheets that were evenly and carefully placed over my face, shoulders and chest. They left only a small area of the chest wall exposed, where the insertion of the pacemaker would take place. To begin the procedure, the right side of the chest area was frozen. As the needle was inserted, I could feel the anesthetic stinging beneath the chest surface, but I tried to remain calm. When the freezing took effect, the electrophysiologist, along with her support personnel began their work.

In the preparatory phase for the procedure and during the surgery, I found myself apprehensive and a little more nervous than usual. I had been through several local anesthetic procedures in the past, but this time around I felt more anxious. Much to my relief, I was comforted by the compassionate care that I received. In one such instance, there was a very warm, soft-spoken nurse that was situated by my side. Every so often, she would check in with me by slightly lifting the sheet that was covering my face and asking me how I was doing. Each time that she repeated this, I would see these captivating green eyes looking back at me. I remember that on one such check in, I could not help myself from making a comment. Unexpectedly, I told her that she had such beautiful eyes! She was taken aback by the comment, coming at an unusual time, but accepted the compliment graciously. The nurse's empathy and concern for my well-being helped to ease the tension in this stressful circumstance.

After working diligently for what seemed longer than it was, the electrophysiologist gave me the good news that the procedure was over. One by one the sheets were removed, and I could once again make eye contact with the individuals who had worked on me. Relieved, I thanked the specialist and the nurses who were involved in the procedure. Although I know that numerous procedures similar to mine are done routinely every day, undergoing it successfully, still made me feel grateful. I told myself that I could not take anything for granted, regardless of how common the surgery was.

Discharge Day

The day following surgery, Dan and I had the pleasure of again meeting with Dr. Chu who came to make his rounds. We were always impressed and humbled by his unpretentious demeanour. Imagine our amazement when he began the conversation by complimenting me on the ladybug pyjamas that I was wearing! He proceeded to tell us that things looked quite good with the valves that had been either replaced or repaired and that the heart function had improved. Much to my surprise, the swelling in both my arms and legs had reduced to almost normal size and I was able to swallow solid foods much better. After a long and at times gruelling process, both his goals and my personal goals had been fulfilled. Finally, Dr. Chu was pleased to report that I could be discharged the following day. I was elated!

Soon after Dr. Chu headed off to meet with his next patient, Dan and I were left with feelings of sheer relief, joy and fulfillment with the outcome of our battle. When Dan stepped out of my room, I sat on my bed and reflected. I pondered what had transpired in the eleven nights that I spent in the CSRU followed by the ten nights on the cardiac care floor. In my time of reflection, there were three thoughts that resonated with me.

Firstly, once I was discharged from the CSRU and entered the Cardiac Care floor, I found myself at peace. It is important to recognize that finding peace is not something that can be forced, it is simply a state of being. Attaining that peace of mind affirmed that my battle was all worthwhile for me and my loved ones. Barring a few exceptions, during my time on the cardiac floor, my emotional state was in a place of calm. That feeling of calmness led me to look forward to recuperating and to making a comeback. In essence, the peace and serenity that I felt around me gave me hope.

Secondly, I was surrounded by so many guardian angels on Earth. Whether it was rushing urgently to my bedside, providing medical expertise, or simply holding my hand, they were there caring and looking out for me. I felt blessed that they came into my life at a time that I was weakened and defenseless. They were there when I needed them most.

Thirdly, I thought of the pivotal role that family and friends, especially Dan, Jenna and Justin played in helping me climb this mountain. The peaks and valleys that my entire family experienced could only be understood by those that walked in similar shoes. Day in and day out, whether in person or in thought, they were there, and I could feel their love and support.

In summary, all the special people, healthcare staff, family and friends that helped me to get to that point were truly my inspiration.

The next day on January 12, before being discharged, Dan and I were given final instructions, along with medication and nutrition requirements. We were also informed of follow-up appointments, and I was given a referral to the Cardiac Rehabilitation Centre in Windsor. My bags were packed, and we were ready to be released. I took a last glance around my room and I spotted the white board that ten days ago displayed my goals. It now read, 'Discharge Day!' I nodded with a smile and said to myself, "It certainly is." I left the room then looked up and down the long, familiar hallway. I took my final walk through the hospital corridor that I had frequently trekked. As I expressed my final thank you and goodbyes, I could not help but to feel so grateful, relieved and proud. After all that I had been through, I modestly thought, "I made it."

When Dan and I arrived at the hospital lobby, I waited for him to pick up the car. Now alone, I looked around and noticed how different the lobby looked from three weeks ago. It was no longer neatly decorated for Christmas. Long gone were the holiday gifts and treasures in the gift shop. I looked toward the hospital entrance and recalled walking in that early December morning with anxious and nervous feelings of uncertainty. Unlike then, I was now leaving with a sense of belief. They say that it's always darkest before dawn. I knew I faced a long road ahead, but for the moment, I felt I had seen dawn. On that note, I prepared myself for the journey home.

Forging Ahead

On my 'road to betterment,' the path would be slow and difficult at times requiring a great deal of patience along the way. Dan and I were often reminded by my healthcare team that it would take time to recover due to the complex nature of the surgery that took place. Patiently, I worked through my physiotherapy sessions and through my cardio exercises on the cardiac care floor. Step by step, making small improvements each day, I could see that I was slowly forging ahead. Three times daily, my ten minute walks became 15 minute walks then 20 minute walks all the while improving my speed, endurance and mobility. With much diligence, perseverance and continued patience, it was satisfying to be making even some degree of progress. In this case, the old adage rang true that slow and steady wins the race.

I was eternally grateful for the support of my family. This is one of very few hospital pictures as my family knew that I was opposed to being photographed when I was not well.

During my entire time on the cardiac care floor, I was fortunate and deeply grateful to receive such excellent care from the doctors, the nurses and the support staff. Dan and I wanted to show our deep gratitude for all they had done for us. So the day of my discharge, Dan picked up some baked goods and treats for the staffs on both the Cardiac Care floor and the CSRU. In addition, I slowly wrote thank you cards to both staffs as well. Seeing as I had not regained full strength and I was still very weak, my writing was extremely laboured and shaky, but I persisted. Finally, I was able to formulate my thoughts and get the words down on paper. Our small tokens of appreciation were now ready to be delivered.

Dan and I began our deliveries with the staff on the Cardiac Care floor and we gave our gifts of gratitude to the charge nurse so that she could distribute them to the rest of the staff. Next, we proceeded to the CSRU, a unit that was only vaguely familiar to me, even though I had spent 11 days there. When we approached the area, Dan briefly showed me around. He brought me to the waiting room where he and my family would keep vigil day after day. He introduced me to a few of my nurses and support staff who cared so diligently for me. Each time I met someone new, I nervously asked them if I had treated them rudely. They chuckled and denied it and I only hoped that they were telling the truth. Also, they could not believe how far I had come from those difficult and intense days in the ICU. I hoped that my case gave the healthcare team a sense of fulfillment for work well done. Essentially, I wanted them to recognize the fruits of their labour.

As an aside, after reviewing my surgeon's discharge notes, correspondingly I felt a sense of satisfaction and confidence upon reading the summary section that stated, "overall, we are very pleased with how Belinda has recovered following her triple valve surgery and coronary artery bypass."

I could not have been more grateful, and I believed that the optimal way to show my gratitude would be to continue my recovery where the healthcare staff left off. I wanted to take ownership for my recuperation and to be responsible for following the discharge instructions set out for me. This would include keeping active and conserving energy when needed. I wanted to accomplish the things that were within my control as best as I could. Even though the healthcare team would not see the long-term results, it was important for me to know that I did it for myself and my family in addition to doing it for my healthcare team.

Dan and I realized that we could never thank the entire healthcare staff enough. Our display of appreciation was the least we could do for all that these well-deserving individuals did for us throughout my stay. They trekked with us through the pain and recovery and through the highs and lows and they did it with such care and empathy. To conclude, our expression of that gratitude was not only our way of saying thanks, but ultimately it was a way of bringing closure to my enduring hospital experience. It was finally time to go home.

Chapter 14

I'm Coming Home

There is no place like home. The relief of returning home and the comfort of walking back into your personal space could not be overstated. I knew the home recovery would be long and would take time, but home was the best place to start.

When I first arrived home in January 2024, it was overwhelming. I wanted to tackle so much, but could do so little. I felt weak and tired yet relieved. I felt frustrated yet hopeful. As I faced my conflicting emotions, at the very least, I was at home. I was now able to control and manage my own schedule. To begin with, a new daily routine needed to be established. This included tracking my weight, monitoring fluid intake, following an exercise regimen made up of stretching, yoga and cardio and maintaining a nutritional diet. Lastly and most importantly, it was vital to rest as needed.

Day after day, perseverance was required through the recovery process. A key element in building strength and stamina was to slowly increase the duration and the speed of my exercise program. Also, I tried to improve my swallowing by eating more solid foods and by introducing more roughage into my diet. I gradually regained my independence by completing more tasks on my own such as self care, light housekeeping, cooking, grocery shopping and ultimately driving. This certainly did not happen overnight. Each task took time. Taking small steps, I felt myself getting better and in turn I felt my confidence being restored.

The after effects following cardiac surgery were not only taxing physically, but emotionally as well. All the while progressing through my physical well-being, it was important to remain focused on keeping my mental wellness in check. This was necessary to help me deal with everything that had occurred since my overall health began declining rapidly prior to the actual surgery. Fortunately, I was in a good place mentally which allowed me to concentrate on the physical recovery one heartbeat at a time.

A further confidence builder occurred in February, several weeks after returning home. I had a follow-up visit with my cardiologist, Dr. Mikhail. Dan and I were called into his office and I was immediately greeted with a smile. This was in stark contrast from the concerned look he had one month prior to my surgery when my health condition was in a dangerous decline. Dr. Mikhail proceeded to inform me of how pleased he was with the outcome of the surgery and with my subsequent recovery. Imagine the strong assurance I felt when he attributed the positive results to my fitness level. The years of commitment and perseverance through yoga, cardio and stretching contributed to the success of both the surgery and the recovery. I must admit, Dr. Mikhail's comments made me feel good and gave me a true sense of pride.

The follow-up appointment with my cardiac surgeon Dr. Chu was in April, about three months following the surgery. This was essential to check the incisions, assess my progress and address any questions or concerns that Dan and I had. An echocardiogram was done along with several other tests. Prior to meeting with Dr. Chu, we met with a member of his team who reviewed with us some of the preliminary test results. Pleased with the diagnostic findings, he reiterated the complex and severe nature of the surgery that I underwent. He continued by crediting the ever-humble Dr. Chu. He then ended by stating that Dr. Chu made the surgery look easy, but it was anything but that. In accord with the doctor's statement, I knowingly nodded my head.

A short time later, Dr. Chu came to speak with Dan and me. Although his colleague gave us initial feedback that was positive, we were anxious to hear final comments from Dr. Chu himself. I was feeling well, and I was improving daily, but the actual test results would tell the true story of what was happening with the heart and how well it was functioning. We could not immediately determine by his steadfast professional expression. However, Dr. Chu soon shared with Dan and me that he was pleased to report that the tests showed that my heart function, the pressures around the lungs and the size of the heart were all in the normal range! We were reminded that the coronary artery disease still existed but for now, that was the best news we could have hoped for. Imagine that. Thanks to the remarkable efforts of Dr. Chu and his expert team, they were able to repair my heart and increase its functionality.

Interspersed in the months of recovery were regular check-ups for my previous breast cancer and melanoma diagnoses. Routine mammograms and CT scans continued to take place to stay on top of my other health issues. On one such clinical visit to London with the melanoma surgeon, he was skeptical about something that he saw. Sudden panic and concern hit me. Wanting to err on the side of caution, he recommended to biopsy the spot in question. Suffice it to say that once again, the weeks following the biopsy were met with trepidation. Although the surgeon felt it was nothing serious, until Dan and I knew for sure, we felt another unwanted weight on our shoulders as we awaited results.

Still recuperating from cardiac surgery, Dan and I were concerned and wondered how we would proceed if we received dismal news. Deep down we knew that inevitably, we would proceed as we had always done in the past. We would push forward and do whatever it took to fight the disease. We patiently waited for results and we hoped and prayed for a positive outcome.

Several weeks passed and still we had no results. An unexpected bleed from the site of the biopsy prompted a return visit to London to meet with Dr. Sugimoto. Looking forward to getting the issue taken care of, Dan and I were also hoping to get my results. After a few apprehensive moments, we heard the news that we were long wishing for. The results of the biopsy were negative! Relieved, we felt confident we could carry on with our lives. Reverting back to the issue at hand, the doctor assessed the problem and then took care of the bleed. We were also given instructions on how to manage the situation if it were to happen again in the future. Reassured, grateful and feeling the weight lifted from our shoulders, we departed for our trip home a little lighter.

One Year Later ...

In December 2024, one year following my cardiac surgery, I was scheduled for an annual checkup with Dr. Chu. Dan and I anxiously returned to the familiar cardiac care floor at LHSC – University Hospital in London. After undergoing several routine tests including an echocardiogram, we would be meeting with Dr. Chu. As with any of my prior health issues, every doctor's visit or every test re-awakened my old fears. Even for routine checkups or tests, my concerns never fully disappeared and this visit was not any different.

Once the testing was complete, Dan and I met with Dr. Chu in the examination room. The connection that had been built with him was deeply felt that day. His human touch stood out when the first thing that he commented on was of a video that had been shared with him. The video was of a dance between Justin and me at Justin's wedding that had been taken four months after my surgery. As evidenced in the video, Dr. Chu was not only pleased with my recovery, but said that the video had made his day! Most importantly, the test results showed that both the treated valves and the heart were functioning well. Content with those results and with my current health status, Dr. Chu advised me to continue living life normally. On that note, I felt the opportunity was there to resume enjoying life's pleasures.

Coincidentally on that hospital visit, we ran into another specialist from Dr. Chu's team who was involved in my care a year ago. When we passed the doctor in the stairwell of the hospital, Dan and the doctor did a double take. Immediately, Dan recognized him as the specialist who was active in making important decisions post-surgery regarding my struggling cardiac condition. Due to my un-conscious state at that time, I could only identify this doctor from his picture in the 'Hall of Specialists' on the Cardiac Care floor where I had spent a significant amount of time in my recovery. On my daily walks, I would often pass by framed photos of many Uni-versity Hospital cardiac specialists, several of whom worked on my case. We exchanged glances and at that moment, the specialist rec-ognized Dan and warmly greeted both of us. By his reassuring smile, Dan and I fully knew that he was aware that he had taken care of both of us.

In another coincidence, Dan and I ran into my former cardiologist, Dr. Shoemaker. In his typical friendly and thoughtful manner, he asked how I was doing following my surgery. After being closely monitored and cared for by him for many years, he showed genuine concern regarding my health status. As I noted earlier, he was due to retire soon, but was still wrapping things up at the hospital. It was quite fulfilling and heartwarming to see several of those heart specialists who were instrumental in repairing me.

Finally, on that one-year return trip to University Hospital, Dan and I made a point to try and see Dr. Bagur. We were keen on letting him know that I had been working on the book that he had encouraged me to write. We were pleasantly surprised that his friendly administrative assistant said that he would be available to speak to us. She escorted us to the familiar surgical area where he had performed my angiogram the year before. When he came through the swinging doors dressed in his scrubs, he immediately gave us hugs. Seeing him brought tears to our eyes. Intrigued by our overt emotions, his assistant stuck around eager to learn about 'our story.'

Dr. Bagur proceeded to tell the story. He explained that he had not been directly involved in my cardiac surgery care. Nonetheless, he was being kept informed and was receiving post-surgery updates on my tenuous progress. In addition, he was hoping to see me after my surgery and before he was departing for his vacation the following day. He continued to describe his visit to see me in the CSRU.

Dr. Bagur had entered my room bypassing the electrophysiologist who had been explaining to Dan the possible need for a pacemaker. He smirked at his assistant, who was listening with interest. He emphasized to her that after all, he went there as a friend not as a doctor, as if that carried more clout. Dan and I chuckled. Dr. Bagur then described the emotional dialogue and the hugs that had occurred, followed by his important question. He had asked me if I remembered his request from a month prior when he had performed the angiogram. He told his assistant that I was still in a semiconscious state. In spite of my state, Dr. Bagur told her that I knew enough to faintly respond with literally just two words – 'the book.'

The heartfelt conversation with Dr. Bagur and his assistant prompted some touching moments. All of a sudden, I was brought back to that angiogram procedure of one year ago. I would always remember his words. He stated that day, "Yes, I am a cardiologist, but I am a human being first." He truly understood our hurt in that moment and he was able to share in our pain. With that final memory carved in my mind, Dan and I warmly thanked him and his assistant for making the time to meet with us. The experience confirmed what kind of person Dr. Bagur truly is.

Forging Ahead

Self Care

Taking care of myself after surgery involved addressing my basic needs including getting enough rest, eating nutritiously, drinking ample amounts of water and trying to stay healthy. For the most part those needs were manageable. However, not only did I have to resume a lifestyle and an attitude that allowed me to function physically, but also emotionally.

The emotional part was the more challenging aspect. It was the self-nurturing part whereby I needed to re-energize, to rebuild my self-esteem and to reconnect with the mind, body and soul. Essentially, self-nurturing was about taking care of myself beyond the physical needs. It was about placing value upon oneself and determining that you are worth it. To provide the impetus for self-nurturing, Jenna booked an in-home spa treatment for me. She identified precisely what I needed at that time. I had to find ways to reaffirm my interest in life and engage in activities that in the past brought me pleasure. This was a good place to start. The treatment not only served to boost my confidence, but also to improve my overall well-being.

Furthermore, I found that social nurturing was very important in the healing process. I had been far removed from extended family and friends for many months. Resuming home visits with these people brought them closer to me both literally and figuratively. Returning to social outings was not only beneficial, but necessary to keep me connected with loved ones around me. I felt a sense of enthusiasm and I was excited to learn about what was going on in their lives. Also, it was important for me to let people see that I was improving daily and that I was doing alright. Undoubtedly, social nurturing allowed me to get renewed enjoyment in life by spending valuable time with my family and close friends.

I ascertained that learning was self-nurturing and more specifically that it positively affected my mind. I spent time learning new things such as reading and researching medical resources about my health issues and about my mom's dementia illness. At a time when I was limited as to what I could do physically, I had to redirect my activities in fresh and useful ways. Hence, I took advantage of these learning opportunities to expand my mind and to promote my personal growth.

Several weeks into this self-nurturing process, I thought about how life can intensify and take on greater meaning. I recalled a moment in particular. I had just completed a breast cancer checkup and I was waiting in the lobby of the Windsor Regional Cancer Clinic for Dan to pick me up. I was still healing from the surgery, and I was unable to drive. I remember looking out the large pane glass window on that colder February morning. I saw the sun shining brightly through the naked trees swaying in the wind. It was a serene scene so simple yet so often overlooked. I thought to myself, "I've come a long way."

In that moment I came to realize that I looked at life so differently. Over the years, I had gained a greater appreciation of the wonders of the world. Taking time to notice the trees, to admire the sunshine and to smell the roses was rewarding in ways that could not be measured. It made me realize that the emotional connection to nature helped me to regain some of the energy that was lost in the weeks before, during and after the heart surgery. I was indeed re-connecting with my mind and soul and it brought me peace.

As I was practicing my nurturing and dealing with my emotional thoughts and feelings, my family was walking alongside helping me through it. I valued their role in providing their presence, the care, the encouragement and the motivation to assist me in my recovery. Dan was the endless optimist yet also the realist. He was honest with his concerns and feelings and expected the same from me. He was continually looking out for my best interests, and he was always there for me. Jenna was the organizer, the caregiver and the thoughtful one. Justin provided the health knowledge, the lighthearted relief and the sensitivity. What did I do in all of this? I accepted and fully embraced their love and support, and I took nothing that they did for me for granted.

Healthy Living

An integral part of recovering from cardiac surgery included participation in a cardiac rehabilitation program. In February 2024, less than a month after being discharged from the hospital, I was referred to this six-month program. The goals of the rehabilitation were to help the patient initiate and maintain an active lifestyle, to build strength and confidence and to take responsibility for one's health. After an assessment by the nurse practitioner, an interview with the kinesiologist and a stress test with the doctor, I was given a baseline score. Impressed by the unusually high baseline figure, the doctor provided a lengthy list of activities I was permitted to complete prior to starting the program. He then gave me the consent to begin the cardiac rehabilitation journey.

Although I was skeptical as to whether I could fulfill the six-month biweekly commitment, I knew that it was a necessary element in effectively managing my heart disease. Each session included a warm-up, a 30-minute cardio workout and a cool down whereby blood pressures and heart rates were taken before and after workouts. In addition, each participant was closely monitored for any unusual developments. Week in and week out I worked diligently to increase the speed and the intensity of my workouts to improve the workload on my heart.

I had an incentive to successfully complete the cardiac rehabilitation program. It was to be healthy for an important event that was fast approaching. My son, Justin, was getting married in May, only three months away. The goal was to be well enough to take part and share in his special day. My recovery was coming along, but I knew that to achieve that objective, I needed to do whatever I could to continue improving. I had to keep on working hard and pushing forward to better my overall strength and stamina. Having that goal in sight gave me something to work toward and further motivated me to heal and to get stronger.

Building strength and energy was beneficial in helping to prepare for Justin and his fiancée, Faith's wedding. Among other things, preparations included baking for the sweet table, finding a fitting dress and coming up with the 'Mother and Son' dance. The baking piece occurred a little at a time and was done with much love for Justin and Faith. Finding a suitable dress proved to be a little more challenging as I was initially looking for a dress that would cover my chest incision. On the other hand, as the incision healed, the scar became less noticeable than originally thought. Luckily, I was able to expand my search and to ultimately select an appropriate dress.

As for the 'Mother and Son' dance, that was another story. Knowing Justin's carefree and charismatic personality, we knew that the dance would not be a traditional one. As the wedding day drew nearer and as my recovery progressed, I continued to strive to fulfill my responsibilities.

Finally Justin and Faith's wedding day had arrived. The May sun shone brightly as Justin excitedly awaited the arrival of his groomsmen. One by one the handsome young men entered our home to celebrate the groom's sendoff. On the other side of town, Faith, her mom and 'her girls' were enthusiastically getting themselves ready for the special day. When the young women emerged from their 'makeovers,' they looked so chic, but they were unable to upstage the stunning bride. On both ends of the city, the excitement and energy were palpable. It was evident that an exciting day awaited us and by the looks of things, we could not wait!

Less than five months after undergoing open-heart surgery, I was ready to experience another proud "mom moment," the wedding of my son, Justin.

The way that the day began continued well into the evening. At the ceremony, as Dan and I set our eyes on the attractive couple at the altar, we were filled with many emotions. We were proud of our son and of our new daughter-in-law, but we were also filled with such joy that I was healthy enough to make it there. The reception was lovely, set amidst the spring vineyards of a charming winery. The evening was topped off with the bridal dances starting with Justin and Faith dancing gracefully to their signature song. When it was time for the 'Mother and Son' dance, Justin and I began dancing slowly to our significant song. Once the music changed tempo and faded into an upbeat tune, we moved into high gear, surprising our guests. My healed heart was filled with joy and I realized that I was present and in the moment of that important event. The goals that I had been working diligently on had been achieved!

On May 4, 2024, Justin married his love, Faith, in Tecumseh, Ontario, Canada. Beaming with pride, I could not have been more thankful for being present to witness this.

In the days and weeks following the wedding, I returned to a more routine lifestyle remaining focused on my recovery. Furthermore, in August 2024, the six months of active involvement and commitment to the cardiac rehabilitation program had come to an end. It resulted in significant improvements to my physical function and to my quality of life. Outside of the program, I was able to increase my walking speed from 4.5 to 5.5 kilometres per hour. I was also able to increase my total walking distance from two to seven kilometres. At the end of my program, a final stress test score was reported. Very pleasantly surprised by the result, the same doctor complimented me on the impressive improvement in my score. It felt rewarding that I was now capable of completing a full range of activities and that ultimately, I was able to reap the benefits of the program.

On the shores of Lake Huron, we enjoyed a family yoga session.

About the same time that I was wrapping up the cardiac rehabilitation program, I had another checkup in October, with my cardiologist, Dr. Mikhail. Similar to three months prior, he was very pleased with my continued progress. He was content with my rehabilitation program results as well as with my ability to complete many lifestyle activities including one of our most desired, travelling. It was an up-lifting confidence boost to have Dr. Mikhail's stamp of approval.

After obtaining Dr. Mikhail's affirmation and consent, Dan and I followed up with our health insurance provider. The provider needed to carefully analyze my case to determine whether my previously identified health conditions had met the stability requirements. Once doctor reports and medication lists were reviewed, we were relieved to find out that I had met those conditions. My cardiac condition was stable, and my medications remained unchanged. Dan and I then proceeded to do something that I thought I would never be able to do again. We began to plan another travel adventure.

Dan and I quickly captured the moment to plan our next trip together. After some discussion we selected the city of lights, Paris, and the picturesque southern regions of Italy as our destinations. As a result, we enjoyed the striking Parisian capital of culture and cuisine. We delighted in Sicily's beauty and its unhurried lifestyle. The stunning sea views of Puglia and its seaside charm offered amazing experiences. If ever there was a more opportune time to travel, it was then. I was feeling healthy and there was a small window with which to take advantage of the opportunity to explore the world. We seized it. As you know, travel has always been a long-lasting priority of ours and it was undoubtedly so gratifying to be able to realize that goal once again.

Live and Give

As the one-year anniversary of my cardiac surgery date approached, Jenna conveyed a promise to me that she and Justin had made to one another. That promise originated during my time in the CSRU when I was in an unconscious state. At that time Dan and the kids became the recipients of several meaningful gestures provided to them by some kind and caring individuals.

In one case, a young stranger stationed herself in the hospital parking lot where she gave out cookies and paid for each visitor's parking. This was her way of showing gratitude for the successful outcome of her grandfather's heart illness.

In a second instance, several London relatives dropped off food during a time when my family seldom left the hospital, except for nurses' shift changes. Having experienced a similar challenge in the past with their own loved ones, they were familiar with the daunting times spent in the hospital. They wanted to offer us support and to provide us with a thoughtful gesture to show their care. Deeply touched by the compassion displayed in these instances and by the unexpected acts of kindness, Jenna and Justin vowed to give back.

That next year as Christmas 2024, drew near, in lieu of exchanging gifts with the family, Jenna and Justin had another idea. They, along with their spouses, and Dan and I, decided to travel to London. Our kids wanted to personally deliver trays of snacks and fruit to families who would be spending the holidays in the hospital waiting and hoping for their loved ones to recover. My family knew full well how difficult those days were, longing for any piece of positive news or any sign of improvement. If we could provide some degree of comfort and hope to those suffering, that would be the greatest gift that we could receive. As we shared our personal experiences from just one year ago, our hearts were filled to see their reactions and to witness how moved these families were to receive our show of support. We observed firsthand how that random act not only brought significance to our lives, but truly touched the lives of others.

Last, but certainly not least, with the driving force of Dr. Bagur, I made the decision to write this memoir. I invited you to share in my life experiences and to journey with me through the peaks and valleys of life. My initial thought about this account was that it would serve as a guide to help and encourage others through their personal health struggles. I thought it would be something short and to the point. However, as I started recording some ideas, I discovered that I had more to disclose than I originally thought. With that discovery, I recognized that this book would take on a different look.

On that note, I began writing. The actual manuscript got off the ground several weeks after I arrived home from my cardiac surgery. At that time I was immersed in my recovery, and I was grappling with a range of emotions. The writing process helped me to sort through many thoughts and feelings, allowing me to relive my life one thought after another. Apart from this, the entire process became extremely fulfilling and therapeutic. The more I wrote, the more I learned about myself. The more I learned about myself, the more I was able to make sense of my life. In doing so, the book became an endeavour that brought meaning and purpose to my life in ways that I never realized existed.

Final Thoughts

One of my long-held beliefs has been that it is not so much about what you are dealt in life, but how you deal with what you are dealt. I believe that your perspective and your attitude are key on how you approach adversity in life. That is not to say that the 'how' is easy to solve. It is anything but that. Nonetheless, the 'how' is the part that I feel I had control over. As I stated earlier in the memoir, I believed that if I were given a chance, I would do whatever was within my control to fight the battle that I was facing. In addition, I believed that I did nothing different than anyone else would have done in a similar situation. There was nothing special or unique about how I dealt with my illnesses. A positive mindset and a hopeful attitude provided me with the drive to deal with what I was facing and were integral in helping me through the difficult times.

That positive mindset and hopeful attitude are echoed in my thoughts on the pivotal role that medical advancements have played throughout my health journey. A positive outlook helped me to accept that with each new diagnosis, I would benefit from the latest treatment available because of prior medical research and clinical trials. Subsequently, when given the chance, I would agree to participate in clinical studies. Whether it was the trial comparing different chemotherapy drugs to treat Hodgkin's or the trial comparing the efficacy of using diverse heart valves in my cardiac surgery, I remained positive and hopeful that my participation could help others.

Undoubtedly, had it not been for the miracles of medicine, I am fully aware that I would not be telling my story today. Moreover, I feel the future continues to show promise in the field of medicine as advancements are constantly improving the diagnosis, treatment and quality of life for patients. I have witnessed firsthand this medical progression in treating Hodgkin's patients. For instance, the invasive, riskier staging surgery that I underwent in 1987 has now been replaced by more sophisticated and accurate CT and PET scans. Also, the full chest radiation therapy that I went through has become more targeted today toward cancerous cells thereby reducing future cardiac complications. Many more examples exist leaving me encouraged by this medical evolution not only for me and my family, but for you and your families as well.

On an emotional level, the first cancer diagnosis that I received several decades ago in 1987, planted the seed for my personal growth. After that initial diagnosis, with each new hurdle that I encountered, I gained further knowledge about myself, about others and about life in general. In turn, I grew and I matured a little more as I was confronted with yet another obstacle. I believe that I attained greater physical, mental and emotional toughness than I ever would have had I not been faced with those challenges in life. As a result, I felt that I was able to appreciate life that much more and that I took less for granted primarily because I learned early on about the fragility of life.

An important part of my personal growth was remaining true to my lifelong aspirations. Throughout the journey, I was committed to continue my quest to:

- be kind and giving to others
- find joy in others' happiness
- show a positive attitude
- express gratitude and last but certainly not least
- have hope

I discovered that these life ambitions played a big role in fostering self improvement.

Importantly, I have led a meaningful life due in large part to a very loving family, special friends, a rewarding career, many worthwhile experiences and treasured memories. Although Dan has reminded me quite often that we have unfinished business, I feel a sense of fulfillment in what I have already accomplished. Even though I believe that I have a great deal more to give, I feel fortunate to be able to say that I have experienced a life well lived. A phrase that I came across a short time ago best summarized these sentiments, 'The best things in life are the people we love, the places we've been and the memories we have made.' I have realized that those people, those places and those memories truly have shaped the life that I have lived.

Have you ever asked yourself: What was my purpose in life? What was I here for? What was the true meaning of my life? I would sometimes ask myself these very questions, but I did not have all of the answers. Was my personal life experience meant to serve as an example for others showing that when faced with a challenge in life, they too could prevail? I am not exactly certain what it was, but I did feel that the reason for those health and life challenges were more far-reaching. I sensed a deeper meaning surrounding the adversities that I faced.

As that deeper meaning eluded me, I thought back to Dr. Bagur's initial message to me, "You have been a true inspiration considering everything you have been through in your life. I am giving you an assignment. I am asking you to write a book about your journey so that you can inspire and give hope to others as they confront their own health challenges." Perhaps this was one of the underlying purposes of my life.

Now having completed this memoir, I feel that if it can be the source of inspiration and hope for even one person, then I would have accomplished something worthwhile.

In closing, this was my life story. Every written thought and every expressed feeling came openly from my heart. I am not sure when or how my journey will end, but until then I will do my best to live each day as if it were my last. I will push forward, I will battle hard, and I will try to do whatever it takes. Simply put, I will continue the 'fighting spirit.'

Acknowledgements

It takes a village to raise a child. I would like to express my sincere thanks to the many doctors, nurse practitioners, nurses, receptionists, technologists and healthcare support personnel who played a key role in providing me with care and compassion in my weakest moments and in the most vulnerable periods of my life.

I would be remiss if I did not give special recognition to the specialists who had a profound effect on me in both a physical and an emotional sense. I extend my heartfelt gratitude to:

Dr. Rodrigo Bagur
Dr. Michael Chu
Dr. Guy DeRose
Dr. George Dresser
Dr. David Girvan
Dr. Greg Hasen
Dr. Bob Kiaii
Dr. Roland Mikhail
Dr. Gerard Shoemaker
Dr. Akira Sugimoto

To all of you, know that you made a difference in my life and in the lives of many. Thank you.

Glossary

Term	Definition
Angiogram	A procedure that uses imaging and injected dye to show the blood flow through arteries or veins or through the heart
Angioplasty	A procedure that uses a balloon to open narrowed or blocked coronary arteries restoring blood flow to the heart
Asystole	A condition when the heart's electrical system fails entirely, which causes the heart to stop pumping. It is also known as 'flatlining'
Basal Cell Carcinoma (BCC)	A type of skin cancer that often develops on areas of the skin exposed to the sun. It spreads slowly, but if left untreated, can spread under the skin and cause significant damage to surrounding tissue
Bone Mineral Density	The amount of calcium and minerals in the bone. The higher the density, the more bone strength there is making bones less likely to break
Capsule Endoscopy	A procedure that involves swallowing a tiny capsule with a camera inside to see into your gastrointestinal tract

Cardiac Surgery Recovery Unit (CSRU)	A critical care unit in the hospital for those who have had heart surgery including bypass surgery, heart valve replacement or heart transplant
Cardiotoxicity	Heart damage that arises from certain cancer treatments such as radiation therapy or drugs
Cardiovascular Disease	A term for conditions that affect the heart and/or blood vessels
Colonoscopy	A procedure that examines the inside of your large intestine including your colon, rectum and anus
CT scan	A computerized tomography scan is a type of imaging that uses X-ray techniques to produce detailed images of the body
Electrophysiologist	A heart specialist with an in-depth understanding of your heart's electrical system, mainly identifying and fixing problems with your heart rhythm
Gastroscopy	A test that uses a long tube to look inside your esophagus, stomach and the first part of your small intestine
GERD	Gastroesophageal reflux disease is a common condition in which the stomach contents move up into the esophagus
Injection Therapy	When blood testing shows that the egg follicle is ready, a hormone injection is given to stimulate ovulation

Internist	A specialist of internal medicine who diagnoses and manages diseases of organs such as heart, lungs and kidneys
Hodgkin Lymphoma	A cancer that affects the lymphatic system, which is part of the body's immune system
Mantle Radiation	A radiation treatment involving radiation to the neck, chest and armpit areas
Melanoma	Is a dangerous form of skin cancer and has the highest death rate of all skin cancers
MRI	Magnetic resonance imaging (MRI) is a medical imaging test that creates detailed images of internal structures in your body
Multiple Sclerosis	A chronic, usually progressive disease of the central nervous system potentially affecting vision, speech and walking
Oncogene	A mutated gene that has the potential to cause cancer
Osteopenia	Medical definition for bone density loss in its less severe form
Osteoporosis	A medical condition that occurs when the generation of new bone does not keep up with the loss of old bone resulting in more severe bone density loss
PET Scan	Positron emission tomography (PET) scans detect diseased cells to check for signs of cancer, heart disease and brain conditions

Right Coronary Artery (RCA)	The artery that supplies blood to the right ventricle and the right atrium which regulates the heart rhythm
Squamous Cell Carcinoma	Second most common form of skin cancer
Staging Laparotomy	A surgical procedure done to determine the extent of cancer in the abdominal area
Stent	A small, metal mesh tube that expands inside an artery often inserted during or immediately after angioplasty
Transesophageal Echocardiogram (TEE)	A procedure that shows detailed images of your heart through a small ultrasound camera that is inserted through the throat and into the esophagus
Transient Ischemic Attack (TIA)	It is a short-lived period of symptoms similar to a stroke and is caused by a brief blockage of blood flow to the brain
Valve Regurgitation	A condition in which the heart valve(s) is leaking potentially placing stress on the heart thereby requiring medical intervention

References

Belzile-Dugas, E., MD and Eisenberg, M.J., MD, MPH. Radiation-Induced Cardiovascular Disease: Review of an Underrecognized Pathology. *Journal of the American Heart Association,* 10 (18). https://doi.org/10.1161/JAHA.121.021686

Canadian Cancer Society. (May 2024). *Breast Cancer Statistics.* Retrieved March 10, 2025, from https://cancer.ca/en/cancer-information/cancer-types/breast/statistics

Canadian Cancer Society. (October 2020). *Fertility Problems.* Retrieved March 10, 2025, from https://cancer.ca/en/treatments/side-effects/fertility-problems

Canadian Cancer Society. (n.d.). *Survival statistics for Hodgkin lymphoma.* Retrieved March 10, 2025, from https://cancer.ca/en/cancer-information/cancer-types/hodgkin-lymphoma/prognosis-and-survival/survival-statistics

Cleveland Clinic. (n.d.). *Cardiotoxicity: Cancer Treatment and the Heart.* Retrieved March 11, 2025, from https://my.clevelandclinic.org/health/diseases/16858-chemotherapy—the-heart-cardiotoxicity

London Health Sciences Centre. (2010). *Cardiac Surgery Recovery Unit: A Guide for Families.* https://apps.lhsc.on.ca/forms_view/view_file.php?key=j90i7xssen

Lymphoma Australia. (n.d.). *Staging Hodgkin Lymphoma.* Retrieved March 10, 2025, from https://www.lymphoma.org.au/types-of-lymphoma/hodgkin-lymphoma.

Mischler, A. (n.d.). Yoga with Adriene. Retrieved March 10, 2025, from https://yogawithadriene.com

Swindoll, Charles R. (2023). *Life is 10% What Happens to You and 90% How You React.* Nashville, Tennessee: Nelson Books.